The Yang & Yin of

Gender Transition

By Joella Sylvia Laramay

Copyright © 2020 Joella Sylvia Laramay

Printed in the United States of America

The Yang & Yin of Gender Transitiion / Laramay—1st Edition

ISBN: 978-1-953610-10-2

     1. Title
     2. Memoir.
     3. Gender Transition.
     4. Gender Dysphoria.
     5. Gender.
     6. Laramay.

No part of this book may be reproduced or transmitted in any form by any means, electronic or mechanical, including photocopying, recording, or by any information storage and retrieval system without permission in writing by the
author.

NFB
NFB Publishing/Amelia Press
119 Dorchester Road
Buffalo, New York 14213

For more information visit Nfbpublishing.com

The Yang & Yin of Gender Transition

TABLE OF CONTENTS

PART 1:   THE OTHER SIDE   11

PART 2:   FROM ASHES ARISEN   107

PART 3:   THE VAGINA DIALOGS   179

PART 4:   INTO THE HORIZON   223

PART 1

THE OTHER SIDE
Dated: The beginning - June 2017

I am dedicating this section to a few people who stood by me while I struggled:

My ex-wife Christina who tried her best to be supportive to our marriage's end even while I took her husband away. You hear all the stories about wives staying? It's not as easy as it looks. They should be happy also and not be pressured to stay with someone they are not attracted to or in love with any longer.

Cameron S from the WNY Pride Center for seeing me every few weeks even though I was late or in crisis nearly every visit. Thank you for giving me much-needed guidance and support through the beginnings of my transition.

My counselors Paula and then Shannon who worked with me through transitioning, the depression, and the inevitable break up of my marriage

My first ever boyfriend who was there when I needed him to move on from my divorce and then embraced the woman I am as I have embraced him with my newfound self-confidence and love.

PROLOGUE
I'm Tired

I'M SORRY, BUT I am tired. This may be the stupidest way to start a book, but it's true. I do not intend to make this book sound too romantic or whimsical. I wanted this book to be raw as a counterpoint to all the happily-ever-after fairytales other people write. After being on HRT at this point (hormone replacement therapy) for nine months to better physically transition to female, after socially transitioning for over a year, after living for 30 years labeled as "male" yet coveting femininity both consciously and subconsciously, and all the wonderful downfalls of transitioning, I am dog ass tired.

Up to this point, I have literally tried everything to make sense of what being transgender is and what it means to me. In-person support groups didn't help me much. Putting a bunch of trans people in a room and trying to act like it is common ground is no different than putting cancer patients in a room and saying they have something in common. It's not enough. There are too many variables at hand. There are too many degrees of "transness". Everyone's transition is their own and despite some common struggles, nothing is the same. Your life is your own to live and you are ultimately alone in it. Alone in your mind. Alone in front of the mirror every day. Perhaps six times a day. Not because you are vain but because you're trying to see the results of this life-changing chemotherapy that is killing you yet healing you as you try to determine if it was worth it all.

I have tried IRC (Internet Relay Chats) to talk with faceless people until they share pictures of their transitions. They are always so excited and chatty like a high school cafeteria. Their breasts are such and such big, electrolysis is expensive but worth it, and how they can't wait until they get GRS (gender reassignment surgery) to turn their bits into the bits they wanted forever. I cannot relate to any of that either, for I still have mornings where I am not happy with transitioning for various reasons. I have lost my sense of self. I am confused about how I came to be this way and why I even wanted to transition in the first place. I am lost.

I have tried Instagram pages and have learned more about orientations and how everything is a giant clusterfuck inside of a massive grey area that contains no rhyme or reason. A single minute deviation from traditional LGBT is its own definition, and therefore a new letter to the acronym. Posts where kids know that they are a "demi-boy rabbitkin" and no one should judge their borderline insanity because yadda-yadda hashtag acceptance. That free-spiritedness may be great for a fourteen-year-old but not for a thirty-year-old person who was married with a good job and an identity.

Finally, I'm tired of all the books I've read. The works of fiction and nonfiction that only seem to glorify transition, where their problems are so minor to overcome, where the characters get the HRT, get the surgery, apparently sound passable instantly, keep their families, interact like, and with, the gender they want effortlessly. I finally want a book like this:

The protagonist starts out breaking down at their desk at work because the thought of being a woman won't leave their minds.

They move onto a better job and get fired after being put on medical leave for struggling emotionally and subsequently denied return even after being cleared.

"Passing" isn't some magical happy endgame for them but an expectation that isn't easily achievable.

They go out in public and are hit on like a sex object or glared at, laughed at, and/or misgendered because they look weird wearing makeup with size 11W woman's footwear.

The protagonist puts listings up on Plenty of Fish, Craigslist, and OKCupid to find a friend or date and only receives pictures of penises, hurtful statements about their body, bigotry, and requests to perform sexual activities on them.

The protagonist gets to watch everyone else get GRS and slowly become happier before them because their company's health insurance plan excludes transgender care.

Where putting on a female voice takes work and they still suck at it.

Where instead of getting swept off their feet by "Mr. Right" they end up alienating the woman they fell in love with for 13 years and hate themselves and her at the same time.

Where their family disowns them and ends all communication.

Where they begin to question if transitioning is worth it after dealing with the first 9 things and dysphoria.

But hey, you're happy you get to be you right? "I'm sorry you had to go through that". "It'll get better". Here are those ten plot items laid out for you to read. The other side to the "happily ever after" transgender stories that are out there.

I want to tell you about MY transition because I feel I have something to add to these other stories. I am not writing this to be "doom and gloom" or to dissuade people from following their true selves. I just feel that being transgender and the journey of transitioning is becoming too glorified. Let me tell you this, it isn't all catwalks and makeup ads.

CHAPTER 1
I Didn't Know

I HAD NO IDEA what "transgenderism" was, but it happened to me. Rather, we were always together. It just laid dormant inside of me like a volcano. Who knows if it was caused by some weird coding to my DNA, hormonal fluctuations as I was a fetus, or because of my abusive past? No matter the cause, it just didn't seem like I of all people would end up as a transgender individual. I didn't know...

I was born to two young parents who also didn't know. They also weren't very prepared for me to enter the wide world and "ruin their lives." I guess I developed normally enough in the end run. Though I did take forever to stop sucking my thumb, but there was a good reason for needing the comfort as I've heard from the snippets of conversation I've had with a relative. Apparently, I was tossed around and shaken when I would cry, AKA need something. That's all I'll really get into on that topic. I don't want to get too off track with that part of my life at the moment.

My parents passed the newborn and toddler tutorials and I survived to attend kindergarten. Looking back, I feel that I played more with the girls than the boys. I remember playing house with stuffed animals and I was the "husband" or "dad" depending on the day of the week. Even at my birthday parties I can recall the girls that attended but not the boys.

My subconscious behavior to interact with girls more than boys continued as I moved into 1st grade and onwards.

Somewhere along the line, I had my 1st unknown warning sign that I was a female. One of my chores was to fold the laundry and think whatever you want about me (I was a pervert, I was just curious, I wasn't breastfed, Daddy hurt me, so I wanted to be Mommy, etc.) but I found mom's underthings fascinating. I remember wanting the bras the most while I folded the household's clothes and sorted them into their respective piles. I would look at the bras and wonder what it would be like to wear one. I wondered every single time I folded the clothes until the urge finally overtook me. I grabbed a bra out of the basket as calm as a cucumber and slipped my arms into the straps. I looked down at the cups over my flat child chest and squeezed the cups a bit. I remember feeling good for a second, then nervous and confused until finally sheer terror took hold of me, for if either parent found me clad in a brassiere, I knew I would be getting the belt, or slapped/punched/tossed around dependent on their degree of reaction. The visualization of their punishment upon me was enough to keep me subdued in my behavior.

The Other Side

I only tried on her bras a few other times, but the one thing I ALWAYS did after my first experience was to save all the bras in the basket to finish out my chore. If a bra was in the way of other clothes, I would pick the bra off, toss it back into the basket and fold the offending object. This way I got to experience the view and touch for a longer duration.

I do not know if this is a sign of a certain behavioral pattern, but I separate my food the way I used to with the bras. I save the marshmallows in Lucky Charms for last, the yellow puffs in Trix for last, and the yellow Skittles or Sour Patch Kids for last.

My next warning sign would have been in fourth grade when I wanted to play in band. I am a very musical person starting from the good old days of playing recorder in music class. I didn't just play "The Snake Charmer" like a champ, no, I played pop songs and songs off the radio just by listening to it or remembering how they went. Have you ever tried to play "Iris" by the GooGooDolls on a recorder in 4th grade? It's doable, trust me. The band permission slip listed all the instruments elementary school band kids could "play". The students had to checkbox two of the instruments to "try-out" on and have a guardian sign it. I readily took the permission slip from the band teacher, checked off "flute" and "clarinet", and excitedly took it home to show my parents, for I always wanted to sit with the girls and play an instrument that sounded pretty.

You will soon see how I was denied and hold resentment to this day. I feel like I lost out on a huge part of who I could have been. In high-school, I would sadly watch this older blonde girl gently blowing into her flute with plump pursed lips as pure love emanated from her instrument. She always wiggled the flute slightly up and down as she played and took such soft gentle breaths. It was beautiful to watch and listen to, like experiencing a gentle tide ebbing and flowing on a solitary beach with no other auditory interference…

The conversation with my mother regarding the band permission slip unfolded as follows:

'I want to play flute or clarinet,' I insisted as my mother peered over the yellow half sheet in her hands as she stood over the counter next to the stove.

'Why the hell do you want to play those?' my mother asked despairingly. She almost sounded accusatory. Twenty-two years later I could swear her full response was actually, 'Why the hell do you want to play those, are you gay?'

'I…I don't know,' I replied quietly staring down at the floor in shame for picking two instruments I clearly should have no business wanting to play. My life would be defined by THIS instrument selection. I would never get a good job, move out, or get married if I played flute or clarinet as a ten-year-old. Instead I would end up a wino wearing lipstick all over my face and begging for spare change.

'Well those are *Girl* instruments,' she retorted with continued contempt as she clicked the ballpoint pen to make the point touch the paper. 'Here,' she said as she crossed out my horribly long checkmarks and added her own small neat ones to the slip, 'trumpet or saxophone. Bill Clinton plays saxophone you know. Don't you want to play the instrument the President plays?'

Honestly, no… because I didn't give a shit what the President played. I didn't know the guy personally and barely knew OF his existence. I was 10 years old! Yet, I reluctantly took the slip back to school because I was a good little beaten child who did what they were told. I blew into the trumpet mouthpiece and made no sound. The band director then handed me an alto saxophone mouthpiece attached to its neck. I blew into the assembly and made a lovely flat note resembling someone blowing into a conch shell. Saxophone would be my main instrument to this day, though as of this sentence I DO have a flute in my Amazon.com shopping cart to buy when I get paid.

It is something I have always wanted and is now a symbol to me of my femininity.

Hypocritically, my brother A. ended up playing clarinet in band when it was his turn to start. It was a pre-owned Vito that he minimally played. Even though I didn't choose the saxophone, I made the 2nd level of high-school band, played higher level pieces for "solo-fest", played in Jazz band, and played Blues with my friend in his garage and at the Dinosaur Bar-B-Que. On the other hand, A. stayed in 1st level and had to be practically blackmailed into practicing. I used to piss him off and play his clarinet when he wasn't using it to show off to mom how much better of a kid I was. The Clarinet is in the same key (Bb) as a Tenor Saxophone which I had at the time on loan from the school, and it was an easy pickup since the fingering on the clarinet is the same. However, I don't think he ended up as a transsexual woman like me for touching a clarinet.

Perhaps Bill Clinton is secretly a transvestite or something. He will come out to the world saying, "Call me Willamina. I did not have sexual relations with that woman. I just wanted to try on her heels." I mean Hillary dresses like a "man", so someone's got to be the woman in the relationship, right?!

CHAPTER 2
I Didn't Want It

By 6ᵀᴴ GRADE I was outcast from the male peer group. I really have no idea what happened to cause it. Maybe they smelled female pheromones on me, or I emitted some transwoman aura. Who the hell knows? What I DO know is that I learned what "faggot", "homo", "gay", and "queer" meant. Granted, I looked the words up in our classroom's Webster's Dictionary, but hey, I was studious, and when you get called those words more than other people in your class, you kind of want to know what they mean.

'Yeah, I AM happy,' I'd retort with some snarky comment while trying to not let the words bother me. I don't even recall the exact definitions being in that dictionary. Except for maybe "queer" being defined along the lines as "weird or unusual". But wasn't everyone queer by that definition? It wasn't the words themselves that hurt at first (until I learned what they all meant); it was the isolation I felt, and the way the words were spit out at me by my peers with looks of contempt on their faces. After all, as Doctor Albert Mehrabian said, 'only 7% of any message is conveyed through words, 38% through certain vocal elements, and 55% through nonverbal expression such as facial expressions, posture, etc.' He wasn't lying.

'You like boys!' they'd jeer at me. No, I didn't!

'No, I don't!' I'd yell hurt. My voice cracked, refusing to deepen as it remained the highest male pitch in the grade. My voice was never something that bothered me too much (until now). I was in elementary school chorus starting in fourth grade and made all-district chorus every year as well. I sung with the girls which was amazing, because I stood next to this beautiful blonde whose mom (also beautiful) taught art at a different elementary school. I crushed on the girl heavy up to high school until she finally got pissed and told a teacher I was bothering her. What I used to do was play lovey pop songs on my saxophone when she'd walk into the band room. Songs like "Crazy for this Girl" and "Story of a Girl". She played French horn in the row behind me, so I'd use the bell of my horn to stare at her reflection.

She caught me one day.

I got a reprimanding from the principal regarding sexual harassment and how as a high school boy I could get in deep shit if accused again. Fast forward 13 years, and now my hair is dyed the golden blonde color hers naturally was. My constant confusion is whether I liked her because I was attracted to her or if I wanted to be attractive LIKE her (and clearly have her hair color). Getting back on track, my voice was starting to crack in sixth grade, and this warranted moving me to the Alto section with the boys. I was devastated. I was no longer with the girls...my sisters.

I hated the boys' parts to the songs. It was all the background harmony stuff and bored me. I wanted to sing the melody, and of course be with the girls, especially blondie. This other girl I liked at the time who later became a nun played the melodies of the choral music while the teacher played piano. This lack of desire to sing with the boys prompted me to ask the music teacher if I could play along with the piano also.

If you know anything about musical instruments, the piano and the flute are both in the key of C. So, all the music teacher had to do was copy the piano music, say something like, "All you do is play the top lines of each staff" and the future nun was in business. Me on the other hand, played an Eb alto saxophone and had to use a "transposition chart" to read the piano music and then handwrite the corresponding alto saxophone note on blank sheet music. I won an award for my dedication and knowing the chart would help me in the future with playing Blues. In the end run, I avoided singing most of 6th grade with the boys and learned a music skill in the process.

Middle school (7th and 8th grade) was pretty much uneventful. I remained small and was insecure about it. My voice, though finally cracking more, was annoying me for not changing enough like the rest of the boys. I wanted to fit in better, to be reasonably popular, but I wasn't smart enough, athletic enough, or social enough. I was just...there. However, one of the things I became fascinated with was how the girls around me were changing. They were starting to bud breasts and would have to wear bras. I used to trace the straps and back bands through their shirts with my eyes, but it wasn't in a dirty way…I just wanted a bra. That wasn't all I noticed. Hair was being cared for, makeup was being worn, and there were more available clothing options. I wanted to experience that.

I used to state the following complaints about gender until maybe 10th grade:

It is unfair that boys get khakis or jeans and girls get skirts, leggings, dresses, AND jeans or khakis.

How girls had so many different hair styles and all the boys had for an option was the crew cut.

Girls got way more options of footwear whereas boys just had sneakers and dress shoes.

It was accepted if a girl said another girl was attractive but whenever I said another guy was attractive, I got called a fag, a queer, or a homo. I used to explain that I wasn't hitting on them and that they should just accept the compliment. (to little avail).

Girls got to wear makeup and all boys had was zit cream or cover-up for said zits.

My first articles of makeup were a bunch of tubes of cover-up that the manager at the drug store I had started working at in 9th grade was throwing out, and I wore them as foundation. I remember loving how soft and even it made my skin look. My mother used to question why I would wear it all over my face. But I also had really terrible acne to where I had to use an erythromycin roll on liquid so when I explained that I wanted to cover it up, she relented and didn't bother me further on it.

The hidden desires disguised as complaints trailed off the older, I became, since I was more focused on graduating high school to attend college for the degree my mom wanted me to obtain. I hoped that my parents would like me, stop hitting me when they didn't like me, and stop telling me I ruined their lives if I was successful. I didn't get the degree my mom wanted, and she hasn't talked to me since she saw me after I started transitioning.

I texted her after they last saw me and asked, 'Did you know I was different when I was a kid?'

Her reply was, 'No, because you weren't, so go do you and let me be.'

CHAPTER 3
Back Again

THERE ISN'T TOO much to report about my first year of college. I got dumped by my first ever girlfriend whom I figured I would marry. I went home for a holiday and a Green Day music video was on MTV or VH1.

My mother was watching with me, pointed at the TV and said, 'Oh you should do that, it would make your eyes pop' referring to Billy Joe's "guyliner".

I bought a tube of Maybelline black eyeliner soon after the conversation. Whenever I bought eyeliner, I purposely avoided Covergirl. My logic was that it was less "gay". No matter the brand it ironically displeased my mother, for whenever I wore eyeliner she would scowl and say, 'You're all wearing eyeliner again!' I would always retort, '*You* said I should!'

It was also my mother's idea to get my ear cartilage pierced when we were at Myrtle Beach. The story was pretty much the same: we were walking along the beachfront stores and she walked by a piercing and henna tattoo place. 'Oh, you should do that, that looks cool,' she said as she turned to me excitedly. 'Do you want to do it?'

I was reluctant at first. Why would I want an earring? Girls wore earrings. Gay men had earrings and our household was racist, close-minded, and homophobic.

Why would I want them to have another reason to dislike my existence?

'I……don't know,' I said unsure of where this situation was going. I don't remember the rest of the conversation, but it concluded with me sitting in a chair and having a dude stick a needle through my ear. We had flown there, and I slept like crap that night between the earache from the plane ride and the throbbing of my first earring. Now I consistently wear two earrings in each ear with my right ear being pierced out of spite in August of 2016 when my parents initially stated they weren't coming to see my wife Christina and I at our first house. The text from my mother read, 'Just so you know, we expect to see our son. Your father isn't too sure about us visiting now that you're a girl.'

My struggles with my gender identity resurfaced when I was with Christina. I started wanting all the things she had. I was totally in love with her, but it was so frustrating how much stuff she could have to express herself versus myself. I began reiterating the same complaints that I had in high school and it started driving me nuts. I hated shopping with her because I had to stand in the female sections surrounded by items I wanted, and then comment on the items she would come out of the dressing room wearing. It was very confusing for me because I was attracted to *her* and *female* items at the same time.

…Then I started to cross-dress.

I don't remember exactly when it started but I ended up telling Christina how bad things were getting for me in wanting to wear woman's clothes. I remember her saying something like, 'But where would you even wear the clothes?'

'Just to bed,' I replied, and it *was* my every intention.

Long story short, I developed and explored many kinks in pornography as I matured into the sexually rambunctious 20-year-old I was at this time. One kink that I was into was age-play where the adult girls would wear diapers, cuddle with plushies, wear babyish clothes, etc. I found it super adorable and soft. It also kindled in me some sort of need to regress for comfort and I remember breaking down crying to Christina that I wanted to wear diapers to bed. I explained more of my past to her and how it would comfort me, and she said I could wear them.

I now have realized that I also wanted to be soft and nurtured. Perhaps I associated that "neediness" with the "weaker sex" but I can't remember which came first: the cross-dressing or the age-play, but the 'just to bed' consisted of pleated skirts with a diaper underneath, just like the women in my kink.

I started to amass a little tote bag of clothes and shoes in the closet that I dubbed my "girly stuff". How it happened was as such: We would go shopping for her or both of us, I would start to feel antsy in a female section as per usual, and became more unable to hold back my urges like I used to if I saw something I wanted. I tried to keep myself together, but the internal conflict literally exhausted me to the brink of tears at times and Christina would ask me what was wrong.

'I want that,' I'd say quietly pointing to some article of clothing while being ashamed with myself for wanting something female... for being a stupid sissy.

she would sometimes reply with a gentle, 'Come on...' because it was something she wanted, or it was something super feminine and ridiculous like a ruffled dress. 'Where would you even wear that?'

'Yeah, you're right,' I'd partially agree trying to affirm my masculinity while I was also upset for not being able to have it *and* upset at my stupidity for wanting it.

Sometimes I couldn't accept no for an answer and we'd have a little power struggle. Most of the time it would end with me buying said article or compromising for something less feminine. It was especially bad at Payless and I wound up amassing almost as many pairs of female shoes as I had male shoes at the time.

Then and quite suddenly, the dressing stopped being 'only to bed.' I have no idea what really prompted it other than maybe a Halloween one year when I was working at a warehouse pharmacy.

CHAPTER 4
Out And About Before The Purge

THE GIRLS I worked with at the warehouse pharmacy really liked me. They thought I was cute, and I clicked well with them as I listened to their girl conversations. I felt included as they went on smoke breaks and let me listen and laugh. Halloween was rolling around and it was suggested I dress up like a girl for the occasion. I do not remember if I outed my cross-dressing to them, but I felt happy that it was being suggested to dress up other than just 'to bed'. I still have the picture. I am leaning over a med cart wearing a black and grey pleated skirt, black leggings, black wedges, black Aeropostale t-shirt with a winged sneaker that had "Track and field" screen printed on it and a headband in my hair which was very bob-like for some reason. My face was very feminine, and I was smiling. I remember feeling super cute and happy as one of the girls took the picture.

I wound up taking the compliments and my own happiness too far as I decided to dress like a girl to work on a regular day of the week. I was very nervous that I would be asked to change and packed a bag of "boy" clothes as a precautionary measure. I wound up changing immediately after walking on the floor because the big old head-pharmacist was scanning medication cards as I nervously walked in while trying to play off my attire as normal. All in all, the situation turned into him yelling 'You can't wear that here. Grow up' as I ran to the bathroom nearly in tears to change.

The desire to dress more femme stayed with me like my shadow. Some days the desire to dress was so unbearable that I would pack an outfit in a bag and throw in on my car's passenger seat in hopes I'd have the courage to wear it. Other days I would tell myself I was stupid, that I was not a queer, and to grow up and be a man. Yet I couldn't convince myself of my maleness and I wound up wearing my female shoes to class more often than I can count. I had two pairs of cork wedges, one white and one black. They weren't anything special looking back but I liked that style of shoe and always had a pair in my "just in case" bag.

I would constantly discuss the situation with Christina when I was feeling antsy and trying to work up the courage to wear them and be happy. 'Wear whatever you want,' she'd say, 'it's just shoes…'

'But it's stupid,' I'd protest, more-so arguing with my thoughts rather than her, 'why do I want to wear girl shoes? People will just make fun of me.'

'If it's what you want to wear.' Christina would reply. Yet the conflict remained. Twenty years of imprinting, decades of learned homophobia, and decades of being judgmental of everything my parents were judgmental about kept my freedom at bay a little while longer.

The urge finally overtook my resistance as I sat freshly parked in my white- silver rally striped 2002 Dodge Neon SXT. I reached into the bag next to me, grabbed out a pair of thin ratty white stockings, took my sneakers off, and slid the stockings up my legs as gently as I could which more than likely resulted in my jagged ass toenails slicing runs in them.

I then grabbed the white Payless wedges and slipped them over my feet. I quietly told myself to finally just come out and to see what would happen as I took a breath, opened the car door, and clomped my feet onto pavement.

No one really cared.

I got a few looks and someone in music class commented on my shoes saying they were 'something their grandma would wear' but I didn't care. The first thing I noticed was how much freer I felt. I liked those shoes for so long and only wore them clomping around the bedroom, but I was now "out", and it was wonderful.

I wore the footwear often. Then I finally took the plunge with the decision to wear an entire outfit to class. I put on black leggings, a tartan red pleated skirt which reminded me of being a prim and proper college girl, and my black Aeropostale skirt with the pink lettering and the track and field sneaker. I even stuffed some tissues into an old bra that Christina had given me. No one gave me any issues as I walked from the parking-lot to class, and I entered my composition class as calm as a cucumber.

I sat at the front of the classroom because I was a nerd, and my professor Dr. Terryberry proceeded to look at me with disdain. He then stared at the class and made a speech about how we were adults who should be dressing as professionals since we were going to get careers, along with some other cockamamie rubbish about the downfall of society. I got so angry and then very ashamed of myself. He was talking about **me** and using my expression as an example! I went home and told Christina about the speech and threw all my clothes away. In the cross-dressing business we call that "purging".

It was the second time I purged during my crossdressing phase, and I vowed to straighten up and be a "professional". This feeling would last until my breakdown and realization that I was a trans individual almost 10 years later.

CHAPTER 5
10 Years Later

I WANTED TO share a poem I wrote that sums of the childhood to college years of my life before I get into what happened 10 years after my humiliation at the hands of my Comp101 professor.

<u>PINK OR BLUE</u>
do the clouds care whether the sky is pink or blue?
no? then why should you
congrats you're a boy! they say
even though plushies you'd rather play
to snuggle up all close and tight
that's not a boy it isn't right
go play tackle, do it rough
stop your crying, you're not tough enough
but play house is where softer things lie

The Other Side

where someone's pain also makes you cry
it's not you they call and jeer
stop being a sissy you girly queer
romp and run both genders can do
but big and strong was never you
so, you fit in with softer side
preferring to go off to play or hide
it works awhile though nothing lasts
time goes by, you grow up fast
and since you're not like them, you grow apart
gender you've mostly desired since the very start
the beautiful hair and flowy clothes
why you like them, who really knows?
alone on an island faring the wind and rain
trying to be the correct way that's been ingrained
but coveting the opposites' life
growing up alone always in strife
for no one will ever truly know
what makes the warm wind blow?
sometimes east and sometimes west
why you're not like all the rest
many nights you cry and cry
but you must pick your chin up, held high
to be what you want no one else can deny
dry your tears realize you've come so far
for you cannot change who you really are

                9/5/16 -Joella Laramay

The Yang & Yin of Gender Transiton

I blame what happened after 10 years of dormant feelings on Caitlyn Jenner. I blame her, but I don't mean it vindictively. Jenner's *Vanity Fair* cover "Call me Caitlyn" came out July 2015. Initially, I thought her gender transition was disgusting and stupid. How could a grown man, albeit a 65-year-old one, decide that they are actually a woman AND then go about publicly changing themselves? I was raised in a homophobic and bigoted household and those beliefs lasted for a long time until I learned a little more about Caitlyn's story. Until I realized that I was in denial of my own feelings.

Basically, Caitlyn had felt her true self for a long time as she explained that she liked woman's clothes and tried to transition earlier in her life with hormones. This whole backstory hit home to me and I began to feel that I may also be this way. It ate and ate at me until it drove me to the edge of sanity. I started looking up ways to increase my estrogen with the hope that it would feminize me since I still had no idea what HRT was. I ended up with 2 or 3 different herbal supplements, one of which is used by woman for hot flash management. Honestly, I couldn't tell you if I experienced any changes at all.

Perhaps the only thing I felt was that my moods were calmer which was probably more of a placebo affect than anything. Regardless, I felt that I was beginning to transition.

Christina and I went to the mall one day and as we passed by Sephora, I turned to her playfully and said, 'I'm going in to get my makeup done. I don't care.'

She encouraged me by saying something like, 'Go for it.'

The Other Side

So, we walked into Sephora and Erykah, who I bought product from until she moved to the other side of the country, did my entire face: foundation, powder, eyeliner, mascara, blush, etc. I sat and watched as my face transformed from male to a prettier version of myself. Christina sat and watched as my jaw became softer, my cheekbones were accentuated, and my baby blue eyes popped and glowed. I looked beautiful yet Christina didn't say much about it. As a result, I felt bold and confident as I cashed out over 100 dollars on all the products Erykah demoed for me. She clearly was a great teacher, and perhaps I am a natural with application because after only that one visit, I have gotten a lot of compliments from ciswoman and transwoman alike when I wear any makeup. I walked around the mall with Christina the rest of the time with my head high and Christina never batted an eyelash at the fact that her husband was wearing full blown makeup like a woman.

I worked at a Honda dealership as an Internet salesperson at this time and began wearing my makeup to work. I started to connect about makeup and fashion with this woman who pretty much hated me ever since we began training together. I also began talking a bit more to Nicole who did the trade-ins and auction cars because she was young and attractive, thereby seeming like a good person to be platonic girlfriends with. Somehow, either Karen my office manager heard me talking to Nicole whose office was next door, or maybe Nicole was getting annoyed with my bouncy energy, but I came back from talking to Nicole and Karen said, 'You need to keep your morning hygiene routine to yourself.'

She was basically telling me to stop talking about makeup stuff.

The Yang & Yin of Gender Transiton

Which seemed fair. I was there to work, and my joy with my gender expression was getting ahead of me. I was also doing great at the dealership and I'm guessing Karen did not want me to become distracted. The manager of the detail shop called me Kurt Rambis because I wore black plastic glasses, and, like the basketball player, I didn't have a lot of initial talent, but my hard work made me successful. He also mixed it up by saying, "Eiiichel" to me every morning after Jack Eichel was drafted to the Sabres. Hell, I was making a little over double the yearly salary I was making at my previous job as a teacher's aide.

Then something happened to me and I still don't really understand it. The feeling that something wasn't right with me and the intrigue I had for Jenner finally caught up to me. I remember it being a day where I worked alone. I believe it was a Friday because Aaron the IT guy had left for the Acura store, so I was alone at the end of the work day. Suddenly I started feeling super depressed. Like crippling, needing-to-curl-into-a-ball-and-cry depressed. I started crying at my desk for no discernable reason before pulling myself back together, equating my emotions to fatigue. I promised myself to take my anxiety medicine and get some sleep when I got home.

Unfortunately, that plan failed. I took my medicine but was still too shaken up and panicked that I went into convulsions and couldn't calm myself down. My mind started to race with thoughts of self-harm and suicide as I glanced over at the knife collection on my nightstand. Finally, I called 911 because I was too confused/scared/disoriented from the anxiety attack. The dispatcher initially asked me if the convulsions were medical or stress related and tried to get me to calm down.

However, I was already too escalated with anxiety and I just started shouting, 'I'm going to hurt myself! I don't feel safe!'

They responded by sending a police officer to the apartment.

The police officer was a cool guy. He said he was a psychology major and did counseling before changing careers to law enforcement. It showed in his expertise with how he handled me. We were in the living-room of the apartment and he gently told me to sit down on the couch and relax. He really helped as he talked and did fact-finding on what was going on with me. In the end run, I calmed down, and asked if I still had to go to the hospital. His reply was it wouldn't hurt to go and get checked out since the ambulance was already on their way. I remember walking out to the ambulance and texting my boss that I was going to the hospital as the paramedics buckled my seatbelt to the bed. She answered back, "Ok, just keep in touch when you are returning to work." I was overly talkative and kept apologizing for wasting their time to which they replied that it will be a good idea for me to talk to someone and to not feel bad about it.

I watched the street lights through the back-door windows of the ambulance and soon arrived at the psychiatric emergency room. I handed in my clothes and possessions to the attendant who placed them in a large zip lock bag, as a police officer watched me clad myself in their non-slip socks and paper-thin blue "pajamas" over the diaper and t-shirt I was wearing. I laid down on a cot with a crinkly pillow that I liked because of the rustling sound it made, and sagged (more so than they already were because they were 2 sizes too big) my pajamas to show off my diaper. I proceeded to suck my thumb and tried to rest knowing it'd be awhile before I would be seen.

    I started getting anxious again as I laid there. I didn't rest much since it was freezing in the room and other people were being noisy. I got off the cot and began playing hands of solitaire at the game table while watching this one patient who was pacing, looking out the window, and apologizing for starting "the war". He kept frantically asking the attendants if he could call his family to make sure they were ok. He also kept yelling about how he needed to watch the news (not allowed at a psychiatric center) to see how "the war" was going. This other guy was laying on a cot next to "window screamer" and kept telling him to "shut the hell up and go to sleep." The "window screamer" turned to him and started talking about "the war". The "shut the hell up" guy said he was going to beat "window screamer's" ass if he didn't stop and then tried a gentler approach. He kept telling "window screamer" that "the war" was ok and to please just try and lay down and be quiet.

    "Window screamer" wasn't convinced. He ran up to an attendant yelling about "the war". The attendant wasn't impressed. "Window screamer" began shaking the attendant by the shoulders. A doctor or nurse showed up saying they were going to give "window screamer" a shot to help him calm down. "Window screamer" flipped shit and the attendant led him to a room to my left. I was still playing solitaire as I saw them give him a shot before closing the door halfway. "Window screamer" kept on flipping shit

The Other Side

and the staff told him that they were admitting him upstairs. They opened the door and took him up the elevator.

The situation had me shaking my head contemplating if I really needed to be here because I didn't seem as sick as the people around me. I felt stupid over having my panic attack and losing control. Thankfully, the entire *Back to the Future* trilogy (my favorite movie of all time) was on the TV so I became distracted from my self-talk and just sat in a Little Tykes style chair for adults and watched it.

When Doc came off the train-turned time machine was when it my turn to be seen by someone, and I followed a female social worker into a small room furnished with only a desk and two chairs that were bolted to the floor. The social worker asked me a ton of questions about my life and what was going on with me right now. In the end run, I admitted my childhood abuse, my cross-dressing experience, the adult baby kink, and lastly, I blurted out, 'I think I want to be a girl!' before crying all over again. She asked me if I was in counseling and I said just a nurse for medication. She asked if I felt like I was going to self-harm or commit suicide if she discharged me and I said, 'No.'

Christina was never told any of this by the hospital even though she was the one who picked me up, and the psychiatric nurse I was seeing for medication never reached out to me after my discharge. As a result, I stopped going to the place I was going for medication and instead began looking up how to transition from male to female. I discovered this hokey website that has clothes for cross-dressing men, "feminization pills", and "estrogen breast cream". I bought into it and spent a few months and a couple hundred dollars on this stuff while continuing to wear the makeup with my male office attire at the dealership.

I ended my employment at the dealership when I got canvassed by civil service for a job at the children's psych center that I had tested for two years prior. I completed the preliminary paperwork, drove across the state to Albany for the physical examination, and was hired with a start date soon after. I resigned my position at the dealership a few days before I would be starting at the children's psych center and so the next chapter began.

CHAPTER 6
I Start Transitioning

I HAD INTERVIEWED for the hospital job in full makeup with male dress clothes around late November 2015/early December 2015. They used my bachelor's degree and my experience working at a day treatment school to hire me and I started January 25th, 2016. Things at the hospital were going ok. I was learning how to work in a psychiatric hospital environment and was getting used to the adolescent patients. I worked the overnight shift, was fine with being mandated to work overtime on day shift, along with being asked constantly if I wanted to pick up more hours, which I did quite frequently. I really wanted to perform well at this job.

A few months into my employment I had an issue where my supervisor pulled me into a classroom and told me that my makeup was a distraction. She said that I was to remove my makeup and not wear it anymore to work. After the conversation, I walked into the staff bathroom and began crying as I tried to wash all my makeup off. I came out of the breakroom sniffling and still crying as I went back into the nursing station to finish the paperwork I was doing. Little did either of us know that the teacher was around the corner of the classroom and heard the exchange. The nursing station phone rang a few days later and I answered it. On the other end was a woman from Affirmative Action who asked me if I could speak with her in a conference room after the end of my shift. I was shaking with fear and had no idea what I did wrong.

The lady was very nice and informed me that she heard about the conversation regarding my makeup. She said that no one could tell me to take my makeup off and that I could wear it if I chose to. She talked to me about keeping my private life to myself and explained that it was the real issue my staff had with me. We agreed on this. She gave me her card and I drove home that morning feeling better about being able to express myself.

I finally decided to take the plunge in April to transition medically. The desire had finally consumed me enough and I had done research on the dosages of the medications utilized in the feminization regimen. I found an online pharmacy that sold the proper medications and I placed the order but was too afraid to bring it up with Christina for an entire day. I finally broke down and confessed that I researched and bought HRT to transition, instead of blowing money on the herbal supplements and "feminization stuff" off of the other website. In the end run, it was cheaper to buy the legit HRT regiment instead of the expensive fake stuff anyway. She did not accept the idea, so I canceled the order for maybe a week before I ended up reordering it without telling her. She held this transgression against me up until our divorce, but I just couldn't stand being "me" anymore and wanted to transition so badly.

I was hoping it would at least feminize me since I did not have a real end-game to fully transition at the time.

I tracked the package until it arrived and when it showed up, I had to confess my transgression to Christina. She was livid and rightfully so, but I tried to talk her down and I explained that I just wanted to feminize a little and would only take the HRT for 6 months (my true intention at the time). I explained to her what to expect and that it was a low dosage. I didn't really know how I identified at the time but all I knew is I hated the way my body looked. I didn't feel "right" and wanted to look more like a female.

It is now 5/27/17 and I have been on HRT 1 year and 29 days. The changes I was seeing were immense, the struggles were there, but I was finally at peace with becoming Joella Sylvia.

But it wasn't that easy...

By July 2016, my body changes were noticeable and by August I had small breasts forming where before I had some pectoral muscles from the days of working out at the gym trying to be more muscular and "male". It honestly crept up on me. I had a picture of me shirtless holding my husky puppy on the bed and cocked my head to look more closely at it.

"Are those boobs or pecs?" I asked Christina astonished.

"Those are breasts," she replied looking at the picture and then at me with a horrified expression.

"No...those are just pecs and the way I'm sitting," I responded doubtfully.

"No, those are definitely boobs," she responded.

"It can't be, why didn't I notice it before? It's not even a high dosage," I said frantically. "I think it's time to stop."

I didn't stop taking the hormone therapy and the relationship with Christina was changing. I think that picture made her pay more attention to my bodily changes, and recognize that she was a helpless observer. I was afraid of losing her, and I tried reassuring her that I was going to stop taking the hormone therapy. However, I began feeling happy with the changes. I felt in control of my life. I was finally doing something for myself to be myself.

It was at the end August that I decided transitioning was necessary for my happiness. I would transition regardless of how far I thought I was going to go, and I needed real medical treatment instead of paying sixty dollars a month for HRT shipped in from India.

I decided to be smart financially and medically. The WNY Pride Center showed up on my Google search as a place to seek advice on LGBT issues. Seeing as how I was transgender to whatever degree, I showed up to talk to someone.

I had made an appointment and was invited to see Cameron S, a transgender expert at the Pride Center. I was distraught and scared as I looked up at the 1800's building with its rainbow flag and transgender pride flag waving in the breeze. Yet another side of me felt welcomed and at peace. Perhaps my fear stemmed from being in a place I felt was "disgusting" or "gay" in my parental rearing, and the feeling of being something "weird" or outcast returning from childhood. Christina came with me for the appointment and I was also worried of how she would handle my desire to continue transitioning.

'I have something for coming in today,' Cameron said as he opened one of his desk drawers. He flashed a tube of pink lip-gloss in its unmarred package in front of me. My eyes lit up with glee and it made my day after a work shift of dreading this appointment.

'I can have that?' I whispered excitedly.

'It's yours if you'd like,' Cameron replied with a smile. 'Let's go downstairs and get the Pride Magazine for you.' I gently took the lip-gloss and zipped it into my black and blue plaid Vera Bradley hipster and followed Cameron down the stairs. Christina was sitting and staring at a fish tank while pretending not to notice the two of us. Cameron and I chatted briefly while he showed me the event page in the magazine.

'Well if you're all set, I hope you have a good day,' Cameron concluded. I nodded shaking my platinum blonde bangs out of my made-up baby blue eyes. 'I don't know if you shake hands or hug...' Cameron trailed off questionably.

'How about both?' I replied happily.

The lip-gloss meant so much to me and I was very satisfied with our meeting. Cameron mentioned the doctor I currently see for the monitoring of my HRT and I made an appointment to see her not long after. Christina, on the other hand, was not joyed at all with my meeting.

I began feeling very guilty and ashamed to see her so distraught as we walked back to the car. She was crying when we left the Pride

Center and I didn't respond well to her when she asked me what Cameron and I talked about.

'It doesn't matter,' I responded vehemently. I was mad at myself for causing her pain. I was scared that I was going to become someone I knew nothing about, and I was feeling burned out from working so much overtime. I was also tired of discussing over and over what my initial intent of transitioning was and was sick of the guilt.

I had my initial HRT consult with the gynecologist soon after. They are a clinic that does "informed consent" for transgender care, so I had to read through information on the medication effects and sign off that I understood the risks involved in taking them. I quickly skimmed the paperwork and signed it because at this point, I was 4 months in on taking them and knew all about the medications. I came home a bundle of nervous energy about starting HRT under the care of someone and made a joke to Christina about growing huge boobs which obviously did not go over well. Looking back, I should have just admitted it to her (and myself) that I wanted to fully transition. I was in denial only because I feared losing her and I was scared on how I was going to change. There is no roadmap with HRT. The doctor cannot take a picture of you and manipulate it like the police do with kidnap victims and say, "This is what you'll look like 2 years from now." The end results are part how you look before you start, part genetics, part lifestyle, and part luck.

I was complimented on my makeup the following night from a girl at the drive-thru of the McDonald's I frequented often before my night shift.

'Are you wearing blue eye-shadow or is that all eyeliner,' she asked leaning out the window.

'I did eye-shadow up top and eyeliner on the bottom,' I replied with a hint of pride in my voice.

'Oh wow, I love the blue. It blends in really well,' she replied genuinely.

'Thanks!' I responded happily.

'Have a good night,' she said as I put my car into drive.

'You too!' I replied feeling richer than the cheap fast food sitting on my passenger's seat.

On 8/12/16, I journaled about not changing into a pretty girl quickly enough. I wanted to shop a lot more for female clothes and accessories because I was making the money to afford it. However, I began to feel the rift in the relationship as I became more emotionally needy while Christina was still herself. I described her as, 'being tough and independent as always.'

I wrote: 'I'm at the point where for work-life I'm ok dressing 'boyish' to keep my job. However, outside of work I feel almost out of my cocoon. What keeps me in? Fears always fears.'

The volume of overtime hours that I was raking in at work were exhausting me, and my swirling of emotions regarding my transition were not doing me any favors. I was bouncing around the idea of voice classes to create a more feminine voice for myself for there's nothing worse than sounding like a gruff man yet wearing female garb and makeup. I asked Cameron at one of our sessions if he knew anyone who could help, and he wrote down the name of a voice coach who helps male to females.

I contacted the voice coach and signed up for sessions. She emailed me a bunch of study material and practice materials along with instructions on how to log in for the private sessions. It was a video transmission and I enjoyed taking the classes. Before we got down to business with our first session, the voice coach explained that there is more to speaking as female-sounding than just pitch. She explained that it is very difficult to learn to keep the voice in your head and then she joked around how you can't just run around talking in falsetto and think you will sound female. She said that women and men also use different colors of language and verbal expression.

I haphazardly skimmed the warm-up exercises and sometimes practiced, but I really wasn't super dedicated to changing my voice. I was mostly doing it because I felt that as a transwoman, I *had* to change my voice; and although a part of me did want to speak more feminine, part of me was too used to the voice that I used for chorus, the shower, and my friend's garage band we had for a few years. Christina seemed to be on the same page regarding me taking the classes in the beginning. She'd hang out on the couch and watch, or do stuff on her phone, tablet, or laptop. We even had a nickname for the coach and would joke around before I had to log-in.

However, I started noticing some changes in my pitch and delivery after the second or third session. I journaled afterwards, "Maybe I'll go back to the days where I was the only boy in the soprano section with all the girls." I would have a session every 4 weeks and took seven or eight classes total before the financial burden outweighed the other transitioning necessities like electrolysis, makeup, more electrolysis, and hormones.

Christina's attitude towards the voice classes changed as I began using my "Joella voice" more and more around the house and then in public. She stated that her and I are, "done talking about trans stuff." The match that ignited the powder keg happened one day when we were cuddling in bed before we planned on running errands. She lazily asked me what I was doing on my phone. I was trying to find some applications that would help me continue with female voice-work without the monthly expense. However, I knew explaining that to her would only incite an argument, and instead I shielded my phone and told her to leave me alone. Of course, that just made her angry and she erupted into a tirade and called me an "asshole". She started crying while she was screaming at me and we continued yelling as were getting into the car. She said she was "so fed up with me" and even yelled at me to get out of the car when we were at the end of our street. I had a headache for almost eight hours after that. "Sometimes I wonder why we put up with each other," I wrote that night.

I felt like I was on a rollercoaster. I still loved Christina, but I wanted to feel better with my body, expression, etc. There was no plausible way the two things could co-exist.

I didn't leave the car when she told me to, and we ended up getting hair color at Sally's Beauty Supplies. Christina picked out a plum red, and it looked sexy on her. In my journal that night I wrote, "I mean it's *sexy*." I continued with, "I hope she goes back to a spunky skater girl". I wanted our loving relationship back when we were younger. We were great friends and perhaps that's all we ever were.

Christina helped me dye my hair. I had picked out a lighter golden blonde and it looked so pretty! I wrote that, "I felt like a beautiful woman all slim, naked and hairless as I covered myself in the suds and scent from the new shampoo the lady suggested I buy." Christina stated she was ok with Joella being her best friend, and I replied that I was ok being J. and Joella if both sides could exist. I reflected on her statement further that night in my journal. "I **refuse** to not be her. The lingerie, make-up, clothes are all things I have always desired and I will expand my wardrobe a tad more. Both sides love Christina and want to be with her. I'll do my best to balance them to what side Christina wants." It was nice to hear her acknowledge my duality and she seemed content with our decision as she was dying my hair, "I don't want my best friend to look bad and certainly not my husband." I loved her so much and wanted to be able to be both sides with her.

I received a compliment on my hair from the night nurse at work. She said that it looked pretty. I giggled with joy after her compliment. As I monitored the halls on my shift, I drew a yin-yang with one side meant to be pink and one side blue with a Mars arrow coming from it. It was meant to be a future tattoo, and showed that at this point I was probably ok with being a male if I had some female expression too.

CHAPTER 7
Disowned

My parents came to visit Christina and I at the house we had just bought August 18th and 19th. The visit started badly before they even left their house. My mother texted me a few days prior, 'Just so you know, we expect to see our son. Your dad isn't too sure about visiting you. Now if you're a girl. You looked great at the car dealership, what the hell happened?'

Her text made me quickly go from feeling dysphoric, to optimistic, and then to guilty. I started an Instagram account around when we bought the house and the puppies. It was my thought of starting a photo album about "adulting" the way every 30-year-old married person does. However, I forgot that I changed my description to "demi-girl" and had pictures of myself in makeup and female attire when I started HRT. In my defense, I wanted to "come out" to them but I didn't know how. The closest I got to "coming out" was when I emailed my dad before the visit if they'd, 'be ok seeing me, now that I looked different,' to which he had replied, 'no worries.' All in all, the whole situation seemed hypocritical but then my anger turned into optimism. Did those four and a half months of HRT work that well? If my mother saw me as a girl then that was good… right?

I vowed to not stress out about their reactions because I was a 30-year-old who shouldn't let other people dictate my happiness. In the end, I honestly didn't expect or want them to come visit.

Christina and I were laying snuggly in bed with myself in a silk floral print nightie/ sundress the morning of the intended visit. Then the doorbell rang followed by knocking. I ran downstairs to answer it, and opened the door using it as a shield to cover my nightgown donned body. It was my parents after all!

'I'm not even dressed!' I snapped at my mother from behind the door.

'You're not even dressed,' she replied breathy but playfully as I ran back upstairs to change.

THE evening with them was awkward. I was sitting in 18-hour old makeup and I was too nervous and embarrassed to look at them. My nervousness wasn't fully out of fear they would reject me for wearing makeup; it was fear that my makeup looked bad and I wanted them to see me at my prettiest!

We went out to dinner at a little diner down the road from the house that Christina and I hadn't gone to yet. Everyone seemed relaxed. We shared work stories and my parents were laughing. They

The Other Side

even held hands walking back and said that our neighborhood was quaint, and they wanted something like it. Christina and the husky puppies acted as a buffer from my parents as we chatted before they left for the night.

Day 2 of their visit seemed to have gone better. However, it was Dad who expressed some discomfort when he saw me from the doorway.

'Why are you wearing makeup?' he asked with a pained smile. My mom stepped in to continue the badgering.

'Are you going to take off your blue eye-shadow Ziggy Marley?'

'Ziggy Stardust,' I retorted. 'Do you want me to?' I asked softly. She gave me no response. 'Do you want me to?' I asked softer and more desperate that she'd say I could leave it on.

'Yeah,' she answered firmly. I felt defeated as I went to my bathroom, standing in front of the mirror with tears in my eyes.

'You ok honey?' Christina asked, 'just take the eye-shadow off,' she whispered.

So, I did just that and then proceeded to circle the recliner my purse was sitting on like a buzzard. I was desperate to bring it in order to feel girly.

After some discussion on our day's plans, I grabbed my purse and nestled it between my small A cup breasts. At least I only had to sacrifice the eye-shadow. We went to a local state park and did some trails. It was a good time, and everyone caught up on life as we talked. I even mentioned that I was losing weight because I stopped drinking so much and they replied they never knew that I had past problems with alcohol.

When we arrived back at the house, they went to the grocery store to pick up supplies for grilling. When they returned, I grilled burgers on the grill Christina got me for Father's Day and we all had fruity malt beverages. We each made a toast for the rest before we drank. I went last, and my toast went something like, 'I know that I'm different now but I'm still your kid and Christina and I are still together and happy.' I hugged them goodbye but was nervous because I was wearing a bra and my boob squished into my dad's chest. Perhaps it's how they knew I had started down the road to transition but I hoped they understood that I intended on working hard and keeping my life intact… But I don't think they ever will understand.

8 days after they left, I received a text from my dad stating, 'Your mother and I understand that it's your own life, but we don't approve of what you're doing. From now on we only have 2 sons until you can be the man you're supposed to be.'

They didn't communicate with me in any form for the following 9 months. I was disowned from my family and it hurt like hell.

CHAPTER 8
The Relationship Between J. And Joella

THE STRUGGLE BETWEEN J. and Joella was escalating quickly. I was constantly fluctuating between staying androgynous/genderqueer/demi boy or transitioning all the way from male to female, and cried at work on my night shifts because I couldn't handle my confusion any longer. I felt alone and trapped in my own body between two fighting forces.

I journaled that, 'In the end run, Joella is more inviting. At least people compliment her.' On top of my internal strife, Christina and I were fighting more as I physically and mentally changed. Did we really love each other? Who's the wife in this relationship? Why are we still together? I honestly couldn't answer her questions but "Joella" was where my heart lay. I was to blame for this too. I had left my wife behind in my dust of nail polish, hair dye, and pressed powder as I constantly discussed my gender identity and transitioning. In the end run, I was tired of dealing with the guilt. The albatross around my neck was getting heavier with each pill I took. I loved her so much, but didn't know how to help her.

I didn't help matters the next day. I was feeling very confident at work being what I called 'a little disciplinarian.' I was in my one pair of panties and was remembering to sit when I went to the bathroom. I felt very dainty and feminine doing that. Since I was working so many hours lately, I texted Christina that I deserved a little treat. Perhaps another pair of panties? She was still so "wife versus husband" oriented that she replied that, 'she's at her wit's end.'

I couldn't blame her. All I had done since I started transitioning was talk about girl stuff, trans stuff, and how I wanted to be a girl, but at least she was happy with who she was and was normal.

I begged her to find a real man. I finished the journal entry with, 'I think we're nearing the end, but I haven't started looking for a new place to live.'

FINALLY, the relationship erupted after a fight at a local hardware store. A Colbie Caillat song was on that we used to really like when we were just starting to date back in college, and I made a comment how difficult and different things were.

'Yeah what happened to those days,' I grumbled.

'That's it, I'm walking home!' Christina shot back.

'Ok go!' I yelled and as she left, I turned away and continued to shop for house stuff. I cashed out and caught up with her in my car about a mile down the road. The distance to her walking on the sidewalk to me felt like light-years. I felt as if we were already broken up. I slowly drove by to see if she'd notice me, but she didn't. I weeded the yard and kept looking down the street to see if she was on her way home. There was a suitcase on the couch when I went back inside, and I heard a "hey babe" from upstairs.

'Do you want me to leave?' she asked me.

'It's up to you,' I whispered as I tried to pretend that I didn't care. I was just so sick of the fighting and the guilt.

Christina started crying and then I started crying, a wailing, hot steamy cry pouring down my face practically creating a pond on the rug.

'Nothing is getting solved, I'm just the way I am, I'm sorry, I'm sorry, I'm sorry,' I wailed. I took a break to try and relax, but I felt this strong urge to self-harm. I had been thinking about it for over a week. I figured that if I scarred myself up, I wouldn't feel pretty, and I would stop being transgender. I also just wanted her to find me, to take care of me, or at least go to the hospital to get myself straightened out. She found me cutting with a small pocket knife and proceeded to pin me down as I was panting with panic. I ran to the bathroom to cut with a dental pick as she bangs on the door. I opened it and she shoved me, and we grappled to the couch where I finally relented. We were exhausted and scared of what had just transpired.

The next day, my anxiety was still so high that I couldn't eat, and I kept throwing up. I hated my life, hated my body, and just wanted to be normal. I spent much of the day sleeping before we decided to pay bills and go grocery shopping. I insisted that if we were going to go somewhere that I wanted to present more female. I tried on my black and white horizontal striped dress, but I was still damp, and my bra straps kept showing. The second issue was that my safety shorts were not staying up on my nice Polish butt. So, I started feeling sorry for myself and emotional. I ran upstairs, threw the clothes into my "girly bin", and flopped onto the bed. Christina came into the bedroom and comforted me by telling me to relax and dry off better. So, I dried off and ended up wearing leggings with short female cotton shorts over them for modesty's sake.

For makeup I just did quick eyeliner and mascara.

Shopping went great. We got like $350 worth of stuff at the grocery store but saved like $100. I even got gendered as female for the first time. We were walking up the candy aisle to get to the baked goods corner and there was an older lady giving out samples of Twizzlers. She smiled at the two of us walking towards her to get to the next aisle.

'Would you ladies like a Twizzler?' she happily asked.

'Oh, that was good, thanks,' I replied after swallowing the refreshing little piece of candy she handed me. The sample lady looked at me with a confused look on her face because I hadn't been practicing my voice. Though I didn't consider that she knew I was trans at the time because she had made my day. I asked Christina as we walked off if she had heard the sample lady say "ladies". She replied sort of monotone, 'Yes I heard her.'

I started counseling August 29th with a lady named Paula and It was going okay. She was recommended to me by Cameron from the Pride Center of WNY since she understood what gender dysphoria was and considered herself to be trans-friendly. She called me Joella at our first meeting and asked me if that's what I preferred to be called. I said yes. During one of our sessions, I was explaining that, 'I don't know what to do about him' in reference to myself. She gently corrected me with 'her'. I asked her if I even looked like a girl. She said yes, and she wouldn't have known that I was transgender. The sessions were $50 each because she didn't take insurance. The price seemed steep, but I needed the help.

When I returned home from that first session, Christina and I got into another argument; the same argument that happened time and time again; that I'm too girly and is this how we're going to be now? I mean maybe?

Who cares? I was a girl now and I was happy. I understood she didn't want a wife necessarily, but it seemed unfair that I couldn't be who I really wanted to be when she didn't portray herself as some girly girl. I figured the dynamics between us would be perfect, but I then started concluding that maybe we were just best friends who slept together and not actually lovers. We ended the arguing by deciding that perhaps I needed more gender-neutral clothes to express this female side of me without going "overboard". So, we looked up a thrift store that we had heard was huge and went to check it out.

I was super anxious at the thrift store the way I used to be when shopping. There were racks and racks of clothes and I felt like I wanted everything I saw. The quantity of their selections was so overwhelming I started to worry that I was never going to see everything. I also started to look at skirts which wasn't part of the deal Christina and I had made in our discussion before we left. Christina took the reins and began pulling plain color woman's t-shirts that would fit me. It was just the shorter sleeves and cut that made them feminine (a style I always wanted). I was also going through the racks and threw a heavy cotton shirt and a short jean skirt into the cart. Christina gently reprimanded me with a "come on…" but I figured I could wear them over some leggings, and it would look okay. I accepted her reprimanding and promised that I wouldn't throw any over the top things in the cart. In the end run, I felt that what she picked was a great feminine mix of clothes that could be "gender-neutral". With that mission accomplished, my final worry was that I needed to wear bras more consistently now that my breasts were developed, and I was worried how that would go over at work.

On August 31st I had my consult for official HRT at the gynecologist's office and I got gendered correctly again. This was the third time since I started transitioning that I was gendered correctly. The nurse who met with me initially before I was to see the Doctor asked me if I was having any menstrual problems. I looked at her and gave her a weird look, so she asked again, 'Your period. When's the last time you had your period?' I smiled a little bit and replied quietly that I didn't have periods. I continued by whispering that I was a boy. To which she replied, 'not much longer.' I heard talking outside my room before the doctor came. The nurse goes, 'Well you live, and you learn, I should have actually looked at the chart. I didn't get it at first, what they were telling me.' I chuckled quietly and grimaced with my eyes closed. I thought, 'What am I doing to myself? What will I do with my life?'

A few days after my official consult, Christina and I went to the mall because I wanted to go to Sephora to get more makeup. Erykah, the lady who demoed my first batch of makeup, taught me how to use mascara better and how to do the popular "cat-liner". We then went to Victoria's Secret and Christina let me pick out a pair of panties. I also got to pick out a bottle of perfume; it was called "Bombshell." But then the trouble started. We went to Claire's and I wanted to pick out some new earrings.

I bought a package of assorted earrings with some basic hoops and some dangly butterflies. She helped me put each of them in and she had a very pained almost angry expression on her face. She finally blurted out, 'I am not happy about all of this,' when she was done as I was happily looking into the selfie cam on my phone.

A week later, I had another counseling session with Paula, which went well. Christina complimented the waves my hair was developing as I continued to grow it out and Paula said that I can't get confused about if I'm a boy or a girl. Today was also the first time Christina called me "girl" or "a girl" during a conversation while walking the dogs. I was starting to believe that my gender duality could work with the both of us.

However, her family wasn't too keen on my increased feminine expression, and her mother left her a voicemail before we met them for a dinner gathering asking if I could 'tone it down a little bit.'

The Yang & Yin of Gender Transiton

On September 21st, Christina and I went out to dinner after I had a session with Cameron at the pride center. The bartender came up to me and flat out asked me what my new name was going to be. This not only upset me because I felt "outed" but it put Christina into a snit because she was sick of feeling like we weren't seen as being in a relationship but seen as just friends.

I became increasingly aware that every time we went out people would look at us funny and we started to be asked, 'Are you together?', 'Is the going on the same check?', or 'Is this going on the same order?' I felt that rift between the two of us, and it was solidifying that the bonds of our marriage were falling apart.

The constant assumptions that we were not a couple whenever Christina and I went out in public was a double-edged sword and I started questioning if I was fully female or just an effeminate male. I was trying to settle into my hybrid mix, or what is called gender-neutral. But I think I was beginning to want to fully transition from male to female. That night I wrote in my journal, "I feel more attractive, chic, like I fit together as a girl."

CHAPTER 9
Ella Goes Out

I DECIDED TO go out to a bar alone as Joella one night when Christina was working overnight. It was September 21st and I went out to a bar called The Underground. It was a gay-friendly bar and a few people talked to me. People said I looked like Winona Ryder mixed with Meg Ryan. I was a different person there. I was a girl. I was Joella.

I talked to an older guy named John. He was probably 45. We talked for a long time about transitioning and he kept saying that I was doing, 'really well' at being a girl. I flipped my hair, laughed with my head tipped back, used a softer voice, and it all felt so natural. I stepped out for a cigarette to try and converse with other people until some drag queen started to critique me, saying that my makeup wasn't done up enough. We got into an argument with the others sticking up for me as we tried to explain that being a transwoman isn't the same as drag.

'But I'm happy the way I am,' I finally retorted.

'Leave her alone,' someone else said in my defense at the end of the argument before the drag queen stomped off.

We finished our ciggies and went back into the bar, and John started playing with my hair and rubbing my hand. I wanted to lean in and passionately kiss him. He was making me feel wanted versus how my relationship with Christina was going towards my transition.

I finally kissed him when the increasing urge overtook me. I leaned in and we made out. It ended quickly but it felt right. We walked back outside, and he said that it wasn't me, that it was him.

He said he wanted penis sexually and I explained that I don't use mine to penetrate, nor does it work well that way because the HRT ruins the ability to get lasting erections. He nodded and said that he understood but I was pissed at him for getting me excited and then abandoning me like this.

'I guess our kiss meant nothing to you,' I snapped.

John smiled and looked aghast, 'wow *that* was bitchy,' he chuckled, and he went back inside, leaving me there alone with my cigarette. I went home right after that exchange feeling very annoyed and rejected.

I cut myself up on my arm with a piece of glass when I got home. I don't really know why, or what I was feeling. I mostly felt conflicted with myself. I felt that I wasn't allowed to be happy in my new body since everyone just rejected me. I also felt abandoned when John left me outside like I did something wrong. I told Christina a bit about the night and she was aggravated. She gave me an ultimatum that we couldn't be in an open marriage which cut Joella off from J. I felt like a young hungry girl in chastity. I had been bringing up the idea of an open marriage or polyamory for a while and she would always reply, 'Well how would you like that if I did those things.' But it wasn't fair. She wasn't two people fighting inside for balance. I was tired of feeling guilty about my transition and expression. I just wanted to be happy. Every time I looked at her, I just saw a failed marriage, wasted years, and it was entirely my fault.

On September 25th I drove home wanting to drink Jack Daniels and drown myself in Benadryl. I was sick of the mood swings, the depression from the HRT, and the depression from Christina being upset about the transition.

We were still simmering about my night out and Christina couldn't understand that my transitioning had nothing to do with whether I liked boys. I tried explaining that I wasn't trying to trick men into sleeping with me nor was I secretly gay. I had a counseling session that day and I had to decide what the best thing I wanted in my life was. I concluded that I wanted my marriage back.

I journaled that at this point into my transition I didn't want any surgeries. I felt fine with the way my body was. I also decided that perhaps I could still be androgynous or genderqueer in my identity and expression to keep my marriage.

Looking back now, it seems like this balancing act was a constant struggle for me. I really wanted to keep my marriage because I loved Christina, but I wanted to be Joella.

'I want to be a girl,' I continued to write, 'I'm lost, and I don't know what my wife wants. I'll keep my voice relatively male if I must. I just had a weak moment.'

I mean, I was trying to understand what I was feeling and to "get better." I was in counseling and doing DBT diaries to track my progress. The future of losing it all, the house, and the dogs would devastate me.

Then I started to get angry. How did she not know that I was this way? I had bought a strap-on for backdoor play between us **before** I knew I was trans, I cross-dressed before all of this, and I was always softer and needier. I kept trying to rationalize how I could be both her husband and her wife.

'Do I want to be more feminine, sure,' I journaled, 'but I don't want to be all trans, she owns my soul.'

Little did I see how far apart we were becoming to be.

CHAPTER 10
Counseling Puts It Into Perspective

9/25/16

CHRISTINA CAME DOWNSTAIRS to eat breakfast and tried to caress or hug me, but I pulled away from her. I resented her yet loved her so much at the same time and it hurt. I resented her because of all the negativity surrounding my transition and how I always felt like I couldn't be who I really wanted to be. My marriage kept me in a box or in a soul crushing trap.

I listened to Pandora on the lawn at my counseling building wearing a hoodie snuggled up in an alcove between two ells. When I entered the building and sat in the waiting area, I pulled my hood up and willed myself to try and snooze. I didn't want to be there or anywhere at the time. I just wanted to be free. I didn't recognize Paula's voice at first. Partly because I wanted her to come up to me and ask me if I was ok. She asked me why I was so happy about the night out and meeting John. What made it seem good? I replied that the attention I received as Joella made me happy and that I felt free to express myself without anxiety of being judged. She asked me to close my eyes and visualize my ideal self. I focused and saw a blonde girl in a dress twirling with a shoulder bag with pastels and other vibrant colors.

'Well what do *you* want?' she gently asked me.

'I want to be a girl,' I whispered and then the flood works opened, and I started bawling as I curled up in the chair.

'Is this the first time you've ever said that out loud?' she asked.

I'm pretty sure that it was the first time I said it out loud and it was the trapped feelings I had about it for months that were finally coming out. My tears were months of denial finally being set free. Paula asked me what I felt I had to live for and the only answer I had was "Christina". I realized how bleak my life was becoming as I continued to transition with little to no support.

'We're going to write a contract and we're going to sign it together,' Paula said as she grabbed a sheet of computer paper from her packet of papers. The contract was to state that I would call crisis services and then Paula if I thought of self-harm or suicide.

'I feel like a petulant child,' I retorted as I pouted and slouched in the oversized armchair that I sat in for these counseling sessions. Part of me thought this was stupid. Admitting that I self-harmed was a sign of weakness. Here I am, a 31-year-old assigned male at birth sitting in a therapist's office making a promise like I'm a weak little sissy. I didn't want to write the contract up at first. I argued with Paula that I was fine, and that this whole thing was stupid.

Paula just sat across from me with that calm yet stern therapist look on her face. My tough guy persona lost, and I finally blurted out my desire to self-harm was becoming overwhelming the more I hurt myself. I admitted that I liked to self-harm, but the guilt afterwards made me want to stop. I self-harmed to show others how badly I was hurting inside because I just couldn't find the strength to vocalize it to my co-workers, my friends, or my family.

I didn't want to bother anyone the way I had bothered my family for merely being born. After a long internal debate and through Paula's silence, I wrote the contract up and I signed it. I signed at first with my dead name and when Paula looked the contract over, she corrected me and told me to sign it with my desired name.

10/2/16
I had another session with Paula and felt proud and happy to see her. We discussed relationship needs and there are 5 of them: touch, favors, gifts, time, and affirmations. I vowed to ask Christina what hers were when I got home and drew a heart next to her name in my journal entry.

I went to work wearing a long college t-shirt, cotton running shorts over a pair of leggings, with my black canvas sneakers. It was SUPER CUTE! No one said anything that night, so I felt that I broke a barrier with dressing more feminine. This other woman only wore leggings with long t-shirts over them so why couldn't I?

Christina didn't want anything to do with me intimately the following day. I journaled, 'my boobs are lovely, and my body is shaping nicely but it doesn't do anything for Christina' She even said that night when we were showering, 'I don't find you attractive anymore.' I understand why she felt that way.

HRT changes a ton on a biological male. Your body fat moves around to fill more feminine patterns, you grow breasts, your muscles get leaner, your body hair grows finer, and your skin softens up immensely.

10/7/16

CHRISTINA and I went to BJs for groceries with myself in a spunky mood. We also seemed back together again. We went to Chestnut Ridge to walk the puppies. Christina got mad because I started sprinting with my boy Volk and wasn't paying attention to my surroundings. This in turn made her dog, Kaia, pull hard on her leash to catch up and Christina was having a hard time handling her. I never really got to enjoy the day and always felt like I was under a time crunch. Paula said Christina and I should have compromised between me walking with Christina and then running on ahead with Volk.

We watched the Giants pitching duel that night against the Mets. Mad-bum was on the mound and they even let him bat so he could close the game out. It was nice to just have a beer, a cigarette, and watch sports with her.

Christina watched me play MLB 11 the Show the following afternoon. Suddenly, my mood started to crumble. Paula and I discussed my gender dysphoria at my session that night. I was having a hard time seeing myself as a girl or whatever I perceived myself to be like. Surprisingly, Christina also said that gender doesn't have to be black and white and that it is more fluid. I think having legit prescriptions made transitioning seem more of a certainty, but I wanted to get there (wherever "there" was) as soon as possible. However, transitioning takes a lot of time and I was scared that getting there would cause me to lose my life as I knew it.

I had already lost my parents and some of my co-workers were very cold to me. My libido was trash and I wanted to be "loved" as a girl. Christina snuggled and laid on me and I found myself more attracted to her than I ever had been. However, I worried the more I changed, the less she would love me.

INTERLUDE

By now in my journals I get to a point where I have a lot of stories and poetry written. I came across a pros and cons chart I wrote where I debated on changing my name. For pros I wrote, 'go by gender name, fresh start, I'll feel correct, I like it better since I gave it to myself, still retains my old name.' For cons I wrote, 'parents and wife won't use, guilt over losing self, work may not like it, have to be woman all the time.' looking back now, I realize that the cons list was basically just me worrying about everybody else and not doing what I wanted to do.

I also did a chart about whether I should go to the hospital.

For pros I wrote, 'take a break from messy house, marriage and work; meet with psychiatrist and psychologist, GET BETTER!'

For pros on not going I wrote, 'don't miss work, don't miss Christina, keep my comforts.'

Cons to going I wrote, 'miss work, wait forever, may not get admitted, can't bring anything, miss Christina, stigma.'

Cons to not going, 'suicide? work will suffer, repeated outbursts, further damage marriage, fatigue.'

I never went to the hospital. I tried to go, but nobody would take me in because they were all too busy. I'm still alive but the other four things I was worrying about happened. My work suffered to the point where I got fired after being placed on leave for months. My wife filed for divorce March 2017. Overall, I was just tired and done with everything.

CHAPTER 11
Ella Goes Out Again

I WENT OUT to The Underground again since Christina was working and I wanted out of the house. I had on my new black with orange polka dotted dress and I had a fresh bob haircut and makeup. I thought I looked gorgeous. I had one or two margaritas at the time, but when I went out to smoke this Romanian woman was there whom I later dubbed "my Romanian grandmother." She mentioned to me that somebody asked her why I was wearing so little makeup. I got defensive because I go for a more natural look and argued that I do not have to get flamboyantly made up all the time because I'm not drag. So, I went back inside and soon I was crying at the bar. Romanian grandmother hugged me, and we went back outside where I just sat on a railing while crying and crying. I was so sick of feeling like I'm not right when I was just trying to be myself.

The Yang & Yin of Gender Transiton

Eventually, I calmed down and went back inside whilst her and some guy argued about Nazis, Donald Trump, and the government. It was too much to listen to. I tried to go back to my writing when I felt a pressure on my right hip. I turned with a shocked look on my face and it was this older guy, probably 37 to 42, with a blue polo shirt, New Balance sneakers, and pale blue jeans. I noticed that he had been eyeing me earlier while we were outside. He had been staring at me creepily like a hawk, and I couldn't tell if it was desire or confusion. I described it in my journal as that he was ashamed of myself being transgender for me.

I had finally spoken up and told him that I wasn't a total weirdo to which he had replied that he knew. As he went in, he held the door and peeked out, staring at me weirdly. So yeah, now this guy was holding me on the dance floor as I confessed to him that I had no idea how to dance. I loved the masculinity that he was exhibiting as he smelled my neck, rubbed his bristled face into me, and gently ran his hands through my hair. I surrendered to it and let this man lead me around like a doll to be possessed and tossed. It was a raucous dance, very energetic, passionate, and sexy. At one point I was leaned against a bench along the wall with him pressed against me as I was helpless against his touches. After a few songs he bowed, and I curtseyed like a dork.

I returned to the bar beaming like Ra atop the Pyramids. I felt renewed and desired. Romanian grandmother commented on how happy I was.

'How do you know?' I asked naively.

'I watched you,' she replied meditatively sounding almost like Yoda prophesizing to Luke on Dagobah.

We drank wine and I shared my writing which was the initial reason I used to go to The Underground. I just wanted to be in a safe bar to have a drink and write. Before you know it, Polo Shirt Guy dragged me back onto the dance floor.

That time it's my turn to lead, as I pinned him with my body, slid up and down on him, and grinding and oscillating my developing hips onto his groin. I was in charge and I was a woman. Soon after that dance, his friends came to the floor to take him home. I'm not sure if they were protecting him from me or protecting me from him since we were both very drunk. Regardless, I was left stunned and alone on the dance floor, suddenly feeling unfulfilled and embarrassed at my antics.

I went home the following morning after sleeping at Romanian grandmother's apartment next door of the bar to avoid getting a DWI. I rested with Christina and we initially had an argument that we worked out and had a romantic day. I threw blankets and pillows out in the yard and we read while listening to country music together. We drank and smoked cigarettes, and I grilled on the grill she bought me a few months prior for Father's Day. She even said that she would have had sex with me out in the yard if it were darker outside. We did make love the next day. We didn't stop looking into each other's eyes and it was very passionate. She was being very intimate, and it felt like we were back to being married in our hearts and not just on a piece of paper. I wrote a sexy poem about the two of us that night. Then the following morning, my life took a drastic turn.

CHAPTER 12
Work Suspends Me

My job at the hospital suspended me for medical leave on 10/15/16. I had told a coworker at the beginning of the month that I was very depressed and contemplating suicide. She had said she was concerned and touched base a few days later to which I had said I was a little better but not much and was considering going to the hospital. Christina didn't want me to go to hers because, 'I know everyone there and see them on a day to day basis.' I had tried a different hospital, but they were too busy to take my case.

I had a meeting with the supervisors the morning they put me on leave, and I confessed that I was having a hard time.

'Obviously I look different than how I was when you hired me,' I began, 'The reason is I'm transgendered and It's been very hard for me.'

They seemed like they wanted me to get better. They said I was an asset to the team and that I would just use accruals until I got a doctor's note saying I could return to work. I was worried about using all my time since Christina and I were going to London and Dublin for her birthday at the end of the month.

'Well what should I do?' I asked slightly frantically.

'We could have just fired you,' the discipline head replied rather staunchly.

What annoyed me the most is that my supervisor Dave, whom I had a decent relationship with, said practically nothing during the entire meeting and did nothing to reassure me that my position was safe. He did not do anything at all to back me up.

I went home and wrote something reminiscent of "Howl"

'Honestly now that I've seen how the other half lives, putzing around meaninglessly like ants, crawling from one dive bar to another it's not all it's cut out to be,' I wrote vowing that I would stop regressing and save myself. This suspension was my wakeup call that my ship was sinking with me the only passenger.

'Sometimes I want to be vomit-covered and beaten in an alley with drugs in my veins. These people choose this the same way I choose to incapacitate myself so that I can RISE UP as a phoenix reborn. Now that I've been out, I will learn to enjoy life as an isolated girl, to be stared at and desired by those my male side feels I am better than. I'll press my size 12 heels to their throats as my maleness and femaleness oozes from this same body. Now that I've seen that EVERYTHING is boring, I'll be Joella but the Joella with love, a wife, puppies, house, and decent job. I HAVE pressed on from this life. There's this limbo of living in a bar with loud bass music. If they feel alive that way, then good for them.

There's death and there's life and I feel at this juncture having seen how to the other half lives, I am going back to reality.'

Two days later I had a doctor's appointment for my return to work note. She hesitated on writing it and insisted I make an appointment to see a psychologist. I panicked and told her I couldn't keep missing days of work, so she wrote the note and told a nurse up front to call around to at least get me an appointment with someone ASAP. The nurse secured me an appointment three weeks out, but at least I had my note and was going back to work.

I wrote, 'even though this all got put on me, I'm going to take charge and do my part to get better.'

A few days later, I called into work to make sure they got my note before my shift started. They said they did but that I was not to return to work…I was placed on long term leave instead. I was not told any reason why I was suspended nor was I given any return date. I contacted my union head who had no more answers for me and told me to stay in touch if I received any communications from work.

CHAPTER 13
London And Dublin: The Second To Last Straw

(excerpt from my journal)

'We are on the train to London! My passport expires this coming February and I'm not sure if I want to change just my picture or my name and gender marker. At the Toronto airport I was called "ma'am" by the customs worker as I put my stuff in the plastic bins. It wasn't until I answered that he apologized, and I said, 'No that's fine, I am a ma'am.' I went to the men's bathroom at the airport and confused people a few times. They would see me washing my hands and leave, look at the sign before reentering. I should probably start using the lady's room from now on.' *(end excerpt)*

At this point I was trying to enjoy the vacation the best that I could despite Christina and I being very distant from each other. We were merely friends on a holiday together. We didn't have sex the entire time. Everything was wrong.

The Yang & Yin of Gender Transiton

It started when we were at The Globe. I felt the emotional strain and it was breaking my heart. I started being a know-it-all since I was an English major and loved teaching Shakespeare. I began accusing her of not loving me while we were on the tour. We were both telling each other to 'shut the fuck up' and neither of us were listening to what the other was trying to say. The arguing worsened, and moods erupted while we were at Madame Tussaud's. The line was super long and that always makes me anxious. Plus, I was getting so self-conscious of all the looks I had gotten on the trip.

Try being trans in another country you've never been to. Try living inside your own head, your body betraying how you really want to look, your voice the wrong gender, as you physically shake, your eyes darting everywhere and physically unable to relax. You are haunted by your looks, voice, and brain. Christina later admitted that it was bothering her during the trip too because she was with, 'a freak.'

This couple in front of us was being lovey and it was making me jealous. Christina said she was being lovey back, but I wasn't feeling it. So, we both exploded. She ripped up her ticket for the wax museum and stormed off. I followed angrily, yelling and swearing about how she didn't love me, etc. etc. which created a huge scene on Baker Street. To her defense I had been tearing her down all day, but I felt unloved, frustrated, and I was in a dress, so I felt awkward and anxious to begin with.

It lasted into the next day until we went out for her birthday at "The Cobblestone" in Dublin. We kissed and took a picture of it and it looked like two girls kissing. I thought it was still a pretty picture. We tried having sex that night, but my penis just didn't work the same way and we couldn't get it to work. HRT really kills a born male's ability to get erections and it will sterilize you. I was at that point where I most likely wouldn't have sex with her ever again.

Near Dublin Castle, an Irishman busted out laughing as he passed me, 'it's a bloody tranny!' I got stares all day prior to this and this last straw made me feel like suicidal shit.

We met the air b&b girls when we got back to the penthouse that evening. Christina said she was tired, and I started drinking gin in the kitchen while the girls drank their punch concoction. I journaled, 'We said hi to Eve and her tall athletic hot/beautiful friend Kira. She has light blonde hair like me and her eyes with her black makeup was <3 <3 <3.'

I started acting "cocky" (I was just being fun) and teasing Christina who wasn't drinking yet and she got mad. She said I was showing off for the girls and went to bed. If I was so bad, I doubt they would have gone out with us later that night but that was Christina's take on my behavior.

Kira did my makeup before we left, and it was hard not to melt into her sexy eyes. We were practically eye to eye since I had heels on. Kira said that my makeup was already good, but her touch ups made me feel beautiful. Christina and I started to get back into having a good time once we were out at different downtown bars. This 35-year-old male stripper was talking up a storm at this one bar and teased Christina calling her "Frodo" and he hugged her a few times. She seemed very feminine and totally different than when she was with me. I was hoping she'd go with him for the night to at least be with a real man...

However, Christina became a drunken mess by the second place we went to and admitted to me she threw up. We finally went to a third place called, "no-name bar" or the "black door" or something and we were all dancing, just four hot girls, four flirts.

According to Eve, some muscular guy dressed as an Olympian for Halloween asked about me. I thought I had seen him quick and mentioned to the girls and Christina that I thought he was hot. Looking back, this encounter was different than the encounters with men I have had at The Underground. Here, I felt more like a complete woman. I wasn't an easier target being alone the way I would be at The Underground. I was surrounded by other women and here was this hot guy who asked specifically about me.

I eventually had to pee, and I worked my way through the ass to ass packed club to the bathrooms. The bouncer in the men's room grabbed me by my shoulders and kept saying, 'leave,' 'leave' and I froze. My brain didn't understand why he was pushing me out the men's room and when people yell at me, I shut down. Finally, I said, 'I'm a boy though,' and he said 'sorry' and let me in. But between the stress of the encounter, the alcohol, the fact that the bathroom was a trough style, and with me in a dress, I couldn't even pee. I also heard someone say, 'what the foock!' ("fuck" with an Irish accent) with some laughing, and I let my dress fall back to my knees and quickly left the restroom.

CHAPTER 14
The Conclusions: I Am Fired

MY JOURNAL IS exhausted, and I have nothing left from the distant past, only the near past. I never intended on this being a long, drawn-out soap opera. I feel you've felt much of the pain I felt was worth sharing. I spared almost nothing from the journals I've kept. One year and two months of transitioning with hormone therapy documented for you to see how hard it was to try and live a double life. J. wanted to keep the house, wife, puppies, and good job they worked for, and Joella wanted to keep the same things yet be Joella. Do you see the struggle? How unfair it is, to transition on one's soul and to want to keep your identity, and yet change it into whom you really want to be? I tried so hard to transition and yet keep everything I had from before. It was a constant balancing act. I eventually lost.

My job at the hospital was terminated after months of being on extended leave status. First, I was using accruals to cover my time. Then I was placed on unpaid leave. Then I was REINSTATED with pay before I was subsequently fired. Here's what happened there.

As stated previously, I was placed on unpaid leave when my initial return to work note was declined. My vacation sucked because I was stressed out about whether I was going to have a job to return to and because I was trans in a different country.

When we returned, I had a note saying that I had a doctor's appointment scheduled with a psychologist from the state of New York to assess whether I could return to work.

I was only slightly nervous about the appointment as I was certain I would be deemed mentally fit to return to work. After all, I had just been on vacation for a week to London and Dublin with my wife, how bad mentally was I? I was fine! My only stressor was getting back to work.

I arrived at the address on the letter which was in a big office park and went into the appropriate suite. I was quickly greeted by a young receptionist girl in her 20s who took my letter and looked confused. She spoke with someone else working the desk and informed me that the DOCTOR WASN'T AT THIS LOCATION TODAY! I asked her very frantically where he was and that my appointment was in a half hour. She called someone from my human resources department to get clarification and a new address. Meanwhile, I was staring at the second-hand tick on the clock above the reception window as time got closer and closer to me being late for this appointment and fired for insubordination. She finally jotted down an address on my letter and hung up the phone. She waltzed over to me and told me the address and that it was in Lockport, NY.

"How far is Lockport from here?" I asked panicked, knowing that Lockport was practically Canada.

"About a half an hour," she replied quickly.

I looked at the clock still ticking away my job longevity above the window. "Well I have a half an hour to get there," I said with a cocky voice that sounded like I was in "Smokey and The Bandit", "I'm glad I got here early."

Could it have been that HR was trying to fuck me over so that I would show up late accidently and be fired for insubordination? Who knows? But it seemed fishy to me as I drove, I mean sped, to Lockport, New York, which was a little jaunt from my former house to meet with this psychologist guy from The State. I should not admit this, but I broke at least 3 traffic laws on the way as I stopped at red lights before running them, sped, and swore in more than one language.

The shrink was in a small office on a corner in downtown Lockport next to an old church. The office had a big semi-circle bannister counter thing with the obligatory monster fish tank, which, as you all know, is supposed to be soothing and distracting while you're waiting to see a doctor who is going to decide your career's fate.

The doctor asked me a bunch of questions about my past. He asked me if I was schizophrenic, a pyromaniac, a depressed suicidal mess, and if I self-mutilated or kicked small animals or babies on the streets. I told him I was trans and had had a difficult time with being this way at first but was doing better and that I ready to go back to work. He then asked me if I felt that this appointment was unnecessary and if I felt my job was, "playing around with me." I wanted to say yes but I replied with something diplomatic like how I understood it was necessary protocol and I was just following orders. I had to make myself sound good.

My interview with the doctor lasted about a half hour after I waited nearly an hour to meet with him in this little closet of an examining room. There was the typical tall plank bed, a chair, his chair and an old computer in a narrow 10' by 4' alleyway of a room.

'I can't tell you if you pass or not,' he said, 'but I honestly think you are fine. You were having a hard time and now you're past that.' I beamed with excitement knowing that I'd be going back to work as we shook hands and I bounced out of the office to my car to drive home.

CHAPTER 15
Conclusions: I Am Still Fired

I RECEIVED A letter from the doctor with his evaluation that said, 'J. is fit to return to duty as a SCTA' and I was reinstated a bit before Christmas. Little did I know that an investigation was in progress to get me fired for social media "transgressions."

My CSEA President Tom was finally in touch with me after I reached out regarding the suspension. He told me there was an investigation in progress but to not worry too much.

I had plenty to worry about, because a month later in early January I received my packet regarding the investigation against me and was told I was being fired before my probation period ended for unsatisfactory performance. My depression inhibited my ability to do my job, my "outbursts", and poetry on Instagram showed someone unstable who should not be working with children or other people because I was "dangerous". And so, I was fired for a bunch of old reasons when I was at my lowest, and they totally disregarded the doctor's evaluation of my PRESENT state.

I collected unemployment for a month before I finally received a new job opportunity. Getting a new job as Joella was difficult for a bunch of reasons: 1). My legal name wasn't Joella it was J. 2) I identified as female, yet my paperwork still said I was a male. 3) My voice work sucked even though I used "Joella" and "female" on my applications which I feel inhibited my interviews. 4) I was transsexual.

To keep collecting unemployment you had to do so many work searches and applications in a week. There were a few positions that old me should have gotten easily but I feel I was passed up for being trans. KeyBank didn't hire me even though I did well on the test and had call center experience. I went through a phone interview before they mailed me a letter saying no. Same with GEICO. Both gave me phone interviews, but I didn't get an in-person interview. I feel my voice sank my chances since I identified myself as, 'this is she' when people called me. I didn't even get a job bagging and ringing out groceries at Aldi. Perhaps I was overqualified for the job or maybe asked for more money than they paid but it just goes to show the hardship it is finding a job as a transperson. Statistically speaking, transgender people experience unemployment at 3x the rate of the non-trans public and 30% of us report being fired, denied promotions, or have experienced mistreatment during employment. I was just one of those statistics.

Finally, I got an interview at Mavis Discount Tire. I had experience working as an installer at Pep Boys and a salesperson at Ray

Laks Honda, so I knew I would do well. I had also just come from a workshop a few days prior regarding interviewing and resume writing. I feel it helped me get the confidence during the interview.

What I liked about Mavis when I applied was that they differentiated "sex" and added "transgender status" to their Equal Opportunity schpeal. I applied for that reason and they were the only job that showed up when I typed, "transgender jobs" into the Indeed app.

The interview went very well. I wore black dress pants, my work boots, a plain polo shirt, and I did my makeup. I interviewed as Joella. The regional training manager and regional head were there and asked me briefly about Pep Boys (not why I left), Ray Laks, and if I could follow protocols. I had just had a mandatory class on resume writing and interviewing for my unemployment a few days prior and left the Mavis interview feeling confident. Three hours later I received a phone call from the Mavis's HR department offering me the assistant manager position. I was elated! I cried while accepting the salary and writing down the directions, profusely apologizing for my tears. The HR lady said it was ok to be happy. I called my new counselor Shannon and left her a message with the good news. I called my friend Steve. Lastly, I called Christina and told her. She wasn't really on my mind even through the good news. I'll tell you why...

CHAPTER 16
Conclusions: Costs Of Transitioning

I HAD MET a fellow transwoman off Craigslist. I had been looking for a new friend, or boyfriend, or girlfriend for a bit now and stumbled across this woman named Jesse. Jesse was a few years younger than me, married but in a polyamorous relationship, meaning they could have another partner that they may share with one another despite being married. I wanted to be that extra partner because I found Jesse attractive and she was my age.

Jesse and I had gone to IHOP for breakfast before I had a counseling session up the road. Christina got mad at how happy I was when I came back from session and meeting Jesse. She moved out of the room into the spare bedroom citing that anyone who I could spend 3 hours with without talking to her first must be more important to me.

That's the reason why I almost forgot about Christina the month later when I got hired at Mavis. The marriage was in shambles and we were apparently "separated" according to her words by early March.

I continued looking for a boyfriend or girlfriend, and little did I know that Christina had a Plenty of Fish profile up to see if she was dateable. We really had hit rock bottom and were as separated as can be.

On March 13th my name change paperwork was official and I was legally to be known as Joella Sylvia Laramay. Christina baked me cupcakes when I came home, and we got into an argument over God knows what. She retorted, 'I made you cupcakes for your new birthday, you ass.' The argument didn't really bother me. I felt conflicted over the name change. I was finally Joella on paperwork, but I felt I was leaving J. behind, that I killed them. There was so much guilt on whether I could be happy with my name if I was married to Christina. The monetary costs of transitioning were also weighing on my guilt.

I was on three different medications for my hormone replacement regiment at the time. The Estrogen tablets were five dollars a month, the Spironolactone to block testosterone and soften up my skin was a tad over ten dollars a month, and my Finasteride to block testosterone was another five dollars a month. Then add in the weekly counseling sessions to deal with transition/marriage struggles at ten dollars a pop and then twenty dollars for the monthly gynecology appointments that I needed to check if my breasts were growing safely, to see how my weight was, and to take blood-work to ensure that my hormone levels were correct. So, let's say I spend $100 a month after gas money to pick-up prescriptions and go to the medical appointments.

Then I started electrolysis on top of all that on March 16th. Electrolysis is essential in male to female transitioning because it is the only permanent method of hair removal and I didn't feel like being a bearded woman in the circus.

What the electrolysis technician does is take a needle attached to a wire, stab it into the hair follicle deep into the epidermis, press a pedal to send electricity through the needle into the hair and then pluck it out with a pair of tweezers. Every single hair follicle…So imagine all those hair follicles on your face and then getting stabbed with a needle and heat applied under the skin to every single one of them. For thirty bucks a half hour you can only cover so much ground and one zap and pluck of the hair isn't enough to kill the hair follicle. You need to be zapped repeatedly in the same hair every few sessions before the hair weakens to the point where it stops growing. As a result, electrolysis is a long and expensive process. So now we're up to around $200 a month total to transition. You can lease an entry level Honda Civic for $189 a month just to put this all into prospective of the monetary costs. However, it wasn't the money that was making Christina frustrated. It was the fact that I was transitioning, and she did not want to lose me. Little did she know that by all the berating, the guilt and shame I was feeling, I had begun to look elsewhere to satisfy my romantic needs.

I put up another Craigslist ad searching for a boyfriend or girlfriend. My initial intent was just to make friends but with the relationship between Christina and I falling apart and my need for love increasing, I figured I would accept someone who wanted to date and have vanilla sex with me. A man named James answered my Craigslist ad and he was different than the dick pictures, old men, and disgusting sexual requests that I had been getting in response to my ad. Dating as a transwoman is challenging because we do not want to be noted as chicks with dicks. Yet we are fetishized by a lot of people (called "chasers") because of how rare we are. We are practically exotic unicorn women.

However, we are not typically looking to top closeted gay men or men who "want to try it out for the first time" as a softer introduction than being topped by a man.

I personally do not want to be the third wheel of your lame hetero relationship that you're looking to spice up by adding me to your bedroom because I'm "unique". Jesse and her wife were different because they are not considered a hetero relationship. Joella just wanted to be respected as a woman and James finally made her feel that way.

On March 23rd we had our first date out to a nice dinner. I ordered mussels and salad with a gin and ginger ale. We walked across the street to the park with a waterfall and talked and kissed here and there. It was the first time I had been kissed in months as well as the first time someone had a meaningful conversation with me face to face. I felt complete as I melted into James's arms and cried happy tears while we got to know each other better.

On March 27th, I received my new license with my new gender marker of "F". I cried when I opened it for the realization that I was new was as real as could be now. My old self was dead. I had killed them off. With killing them I lost my job, wife, parents, and everything that went along with them. I cried for that reason too as I held my new license up next to my old license, flashing my eyes over the "M" on the old to the "F" on the new. I was legally a female!

On April 25th, I slept over at James's place and we had sex that following morning. It was the first time I had had sex in months and this time I was the woman. It was awkward at first trying to get into position as I wanted to be taken doggie style because I am a submissive.

That didn't work nor did a sideways position. Finally, we settled on cowgirl and I rode him like a jockey in a steeplechase. It felt so amazing to be taken and to be held as we had sex.

Christina filed for divorce when I got home from my affair. We got into an argument and she asked me if I slept with James.

'Yes, I did, and it was fantastic,' I calmly replied at the breakfast table.

'That's it! I'm going to file the papers,' she stormed out of the kitchen and began grabbing her purse and keys. She peeked back into the kitchen, 'Have fun taking it up the ass for the rest of your life!' she yelled as she turned back to leave the house.

'Don't knock it if you haven't tried it,' I yelled back as the door slammed. I sat and stared down at my breakfast in shock. The marriage was finally dead. She had said we were separated. She had left the marriage bed in January. We had fought nearly the entire time I was taking the hormone therapy. She had said I wasn't attractive to her anymore. It was clearly time for us to move on.

The Other Side

Through all the hurt and negativity from her I still don't hate her for leaving me. Not many couples stay together during transition. I was a depressed tumultuous mess and she hated the transition while trying to be as supportive as possible. I reeled from her resentment of me and spiraled.

I self-harmed. I drank excessively and talked of suicide. I had police at our house to check in on me regarding texts and posts I wrote on online chats. We argued and argued and argued constantly. Who would want to stay married to someone like that? I have now blossomed into this new person, the person I was meant to be. We both tried but we both needed to move on.

The relationship was over. It was doomed from the beginning because I knew she didn't want to be with me as a woman. I had hoped she would see past it. For while it made sense that she wasn't attracted to women, it took a long time for it to click that I *was* a woman despite looking like one. After thirteen years of being together, part of me hoped that she would be attracted to me as a person first, for what I liked, disliked, my personality, and those experiences we shared for those many years like the concerts, the trips, the laughs and frustrations we shared…our wedding, and not just my gender…I assumed that after all those years that attraction went deeper than just appearance. But even I didn't remember how I used to look. The HRT softened my face, I had grown breasts, I grew my hair out and it became softer, and the estrogen was making my mood, personality, and even sexuality change. I was not the same man she married in any real form.

It always makes me question if being in a relationship with

The Yang & Yin of Gender Transiton

Christina helped or hindered me finally becoming my true self. I think if I were single, I would be a very miserable man who would be constantly trying to validate their assumed gender. Whether through working long hours, going to the gym, buying a fast car, hanging out with my friend Steve, or playing hockey again, I would have tried to distract myself or "teach" myself how to be a "man" and stay one. And looking at all of this, that is what is so amazing about gender. None of that would have saved me. I can do all of that now as a woman and it doesn't make me less of a woman. That's what is so hard for people to understand about being transgender. It's not something you can suppress. You just *are* and it's why ultimately without going to The Pride Center, I would be dead.

Sure, being with Christina helped me transition. I had a best friend. I had a wife. I had a woman…to study and craft bits of what I liked about her into my own womanhood that was quelled inside the inner recesses of my subconscious. Hell, she was the one who put me at ease when I first started crossdressing. She was there when I got my makeup done for the first time and when I got my other set of earrings. I hate needles and never would have fathomed getting a tattoo, but she got hers early in our relationship and if she could do it then so could I. They have nothing to do with Christina and they're not even in the same spot as her tattoo but if it weren't for being in a relationship with her, I wouldn't have gotten them done. Not that I was trying to be tougher than her. She was just so…inspiring with how upbeat, adventurous, and caring she was. While I was never those things. I was a dark, brooding, introvert who wrote poetry and played blues on my saxophone. Meeting her was the catalyst that opened my soul up to living life the way you wanted to live it.

In the end, it was The Pride Center that helped me transition. Christina unfortunately was the casualty as she was my closest ally. Cameron S. at The Pride Center and I talked at least once a month on how the relationship between Christina and I was doing and on how I was handling transitioning. He also gave me resources for HRT, voice therapy, and even GRS. I never would have found how to safely go about transitioning without Googling "LGBT". Thankfully though, I had a friend in Christina to go with me to that first fateful meeting…

On May 27th I moved out due to the divorce. She lawyered up and I gave her the house and uncontested the divorce to save face.

I am grateful she had compassion enough to let the relationship fade naturally and not make it uglier than it was at times. I am tearing up while finishing up this book and touching on this subject. I will always love Christina whether that love exists as a friend or good memories of the love that we shared when we were together. We spent thirteen years together and that's not anything to sneeze at…. I had to take a break from writing just now as I started bawling, tears streaming down my face. James came down to comfort me…Between bouts of tears I will finish this book.

CHAPTER 17
Conclusions: My Parents Are Gone

With Father's Day being days away, I texted my mother after not hearing from them for the following: Thanksgiving '16, my birthday, Christmas '16, New Years, Easter, Mother's Day, and her birthday. They have spent a little over six months ignoring me. Finally, I got a response from her.

> Me: So, I guess I shouldn't have to worry about Father's Day since you're going to disown your own flesh and blood…
> Me: Which is the cruelest thing anyone has done to me.
> Her: Yes, don't bother
> Her: Get some psych counseling instead
> Her: We are too old to deal with your problems
> Her: Cruel is having your son having his head messed up changing into a girl

The Other Side

Me: I've been this way for years I've been in counseling for years. I'm finally happy now and you won't be in my life for something I have always been. You have no idea what I've hid from you in my head and in my heart.

Me: Yeah well, I'm a pretty girl at that too

Me: It's not even an issue you have to deal with. It's not even an issue, I'm just being who I needed to be.

Her: Whatever

Me: Exactly, you have no idea.

Maybe my parents will come around on their own someday, people have said. Maybe they will see a television special and come around, people have also said. Maybe they will think back on me as their kid and accept that no matter what I am or who I'm in a relationship with, that I'm still their child and they will love me not matter what. I have no idea if I am totally dead to them or if they are hoping that this is something I will "snap out of" or that "it's just a phase." Over thirteen months on the HRT, with a female gender marker, a female name, with 36B and growing breasts, with delicious legs and body forming more feminine every week, I will not relent. I stayed the course and fought to be Joella and Joella I will stay. To do otherwise would be impossible and stupid. Perhaps I can send them this book and a mamby-pamby book to give them both sides on the story of transitioning. After all, this is all why I wrote this book in the first place.

PART 2

From Ashes Arisen

Dated: June 2017 – September 2019

I am dedicating this section to a few people who enhanced and embraced this woman that I was meant to be:

My coworkers at Mavis who respect me as a woman and as their assistant manager. Especially Don G. who has been supportive and caring since I first started working there.

My new counselor Sarah S. who I started to see once Shannon went to a new job. You have been a role model and mentor for what a mature, classy lady is like.

My brother Cameron who has kept in touch every now and then to tell me goofy work stories or to vent. It is nice to feel connected to someone in my family.

My ex-wife Christina for still being there for me as I vented and tried to evolve along with our present relationship as friends.

PROLOGUE
I'm Reborn

> (Excerpt from one of my poems)
> …Though sometimes the grounds
> were rough
> she had to keep exterior tough
> for that one day
> when she will stop and cry
> I'm a happy, beautiful butterfly!
> (9/14/16- Joella Laramay)

I HAVE READ and reread what I will now call "part I" of this book many times. Part II picks up right after Father's Day 2017 and has been written in a format like Part I. It utilizes blog entries and DBT journals that I wrote at the time of the events. My goal was to keep the story "in the moment" as you transitioned along with me.

The Yang & Yin of Gender Transiton

If you recall, my initial reason for writing was to counterpoint the happy stories I've read and seen on television. I never intended on writing more, but I felt sheepish about leaving the story as a one-trick-pony that read as unfinished and full of vitriol apart for the last pages where I state that I'm feeling better.

I have confidence now and I do not bemoan the losses I have incurred anymore. Regardless of how easy or hard we think I had, this book transitioned along with me and I feel that I owe both you and me a happy ending to show healing, optimism, and that inner peace is possible.

1/4/2019

CHAPTER 1
Ella Goes Back To School

I CONTINUED TO truck along after my mother's final words to me. I was three months into my relationship with my boyfriend and four months into my employment at Mavis. I was making ends meet with my Mavis paychecks, but I was constantly beating myself up for having squandered my education. I would attempt to reassure myself that technically I <u>was</u> using my degree. I was teaching customers about what was wrong with their vehicles in a way they could understand, and I had to be a good public speaker who sounded relatively intelligent. However, what happened if I wanted to leave Mavis? My teaching degree wasn't very useful on its own and my teaching license had expired years prior. Either I would have to get my master's degree in teaching and renew my license or pick up another degree or qualification to use for a fallback plan or career.

I used Christina as a yardstick for being a successful female considering how much time we had spent together. She had gotten her master's degree and was doing well enough to go on cruises and pay for the house so why couldn't I go back to school? The chaos in my life had stabilized and I had the ability to freely decide what I wanted to do for my future instead of feeling like I was calling audibles.

You figure:
1. My first job at Kinney's was because my mom worked there.
2. I attended the University @ Buffalo because it was my mom's idea for me to go to pharmacy school.
3. I changed majors to English education because my grades weren't high enough to make it into pharmacy school and my English teacher suggested I teach because I was a good writer.
4. My second job at Byrne Dairy was because my mom wanted me to get a second job.
5. My job at Omnicare was because my mom worked there.
6. My job at the school was because my ex, Christina already worked for the organization.
7. My job at Ray Laks was because I was sick of the school job.
8. My job at the children's psychiatric hospital was because Christina worked for the adult facility and it was better pay and benefits than the dealership.
9. My job at Mavis was because the children's psychiatric hospital fired me, and I needed a job. Unemployment requires a legitimate reason to turn down a job offer whether it be a

physical issue, transportation issue, etc. I had to accept the position since I had no reason to decline.

10. I let Christina and my family get into my head while trying to be my true self. I couldn't stop despite them wanting me to.

Therefore, my transition helped pave my way to self-determination and I began looking at Erie Community College's website to ascertain what I wanted to do. My objective was to find a broad degree that would get me into a growing career. Finally, I decided between automotive tech and information technology. I was already working in the automotive industry and I hoped that obtaining certifications in automotive repair would make me more viable for getting my own store to run. However, was that really what I wanted to do? The more I considered the degree, the more I realized that I was again settling on something. I needed to get out of the comfort zone. What appealed to me and had career longevity? I knew how to build computers and I wanted to learn more. Information technology and networking was the way to go.

I registered as an online student which worked perfectly with working full-time since I only needed to go to campus one night a week each semester for my Cisco classes. It is silly looking back but the only thing that gave me anxiety was how I'd be perceived by others. The Cisco classes were four hours long, so I would more than likely need to use the restroom. Thankfully, this irrational fear went away my first night of class after being called female pronouns.

Thus, things seemed stable and I was continuing to rebuild.

CHAPTER 2
I'm Good, I'm Bad, I'm Ugly

THINGS WERE GOING well with school. I allotted each class its own night of the week for schoolwork and my grades at the time of midterms were around an A- to B+. I began feeling confident about my physical appearance and was walking with my head up around campus at night. I got over the fear of my voice selling me out and began answering questions and offering insight in class. I was the only woman in class, and I relished it. I felt empowered despite having been in college already and imagined myself as Sylvia Plath at Smith College. As crazy as it sounds, that imagery gave me some absolution from my anxiety.

My gender dysphoria ebbed and flowed instead of being so prevalent and I wrote a blog entry titled "Coming to Terms":

(10/9/17)

When dysphoria hits, I go into a tailspin questioning

everything regarding my transition from male to female. Am I even a woman if I have my male bits, my voice is mostly male, and I work in a car shop with a male uniform and move "male" in size 11 steel toed boots?

What makes me a woman? My love and decent artistry with makeup? That I look good in female attire? My nice Polish ass? My feminizing body? My growing B cup breasts? My longer and softer hair? I could go on and on. It's all bullshit.

I flip flop on whether I want any surgery. It's expensive both the initial procedure and the time off to recover. Do I really need it to justify my existence as a woman? I don't look bad, do I? These are the constant conflicts raging in my mind. I'm getting sick of it.

Today I worked through it...

My face is enough where I don't want FFS. I don't need implants. I'm generally happy with my body at this point in my transition which I find phenomenal and uplifting. I don't hate my size 11 woman's feet. I still have cute shoes and find my feet soft and femme. Lastly, I don't hate my voice. I used to sing and don't want to lose that. Even if I sound like Rob Thomas or Johnny Rzeznik in a rockabilly dress and MaryJane's.

...Gender is in your heart and mind, it's not a checklist or scantron test.

Things were mostly going well in my social life too. I was starting to become more open with myself and trying to meet other transwomen. Christina and I were still communicating, and I was becoming more used to hearing about her relationship with her boyfriend. She even asked if I had plans for that upcoming Thanksgiving and she said she would call if she didn't have anything to do.

The only real issue was the crumbling dynamics between my boyfriend and me. We were nearing seven months together, but it seemed like he completely lost interest in me. I downloaded the Apartment Finder app and began considering my financial situation.

I began equating his passivity towards me as a reflection on my appearance and "performance" as a woman. Then I would bemoan everything in my current life and hate myself for transitioning.

How could I have thrown away a wife, a house, a good job, and puppies for this? It was a terrible trade-off. Instead, I ended up with a passive boyfriend, a duplex where I didn't even have my own room, and a lower paying job I had to accept because I was collecting unemployment. I wrote that:

(10/29/17)

I'm depressed and more miserable now. James and I are supposedly in a relationship, but it feels like we're merely roommates. There's always something going on with him and he's not affectionate. We don't date, and he doesn't show me that he's even interested in me. This is turn makes me question myself. Is it me? Am I ugly? Is it the diapers / little lifestyle I sort of have? I feel like he's bored with me and it makes me feel unwanted. I'd rather die than be in this relationship because I feel like shit. Like I'm unlovable.

I have no idea why I threw everything away just to be in a relationship where I'm unhappy. He doesn't even try. I'm sick of going to him and crying with my issues. He gives up and doesn't help me. I'm going to school because I'm trying to rebuild my life, but it doesn't look like James is going to be in it.

I don't know if I'll ever find my soul mate. Perhaps Christina was it and I blew it by fucking turning into a girl. I'm not happy. I'm happy that I'm me, but what's the use? I get dick pics, people "complimenting" me by saying how they love "tranny porn", how they're looking for a "passable" transwoman, or a "trap queen".

Thankfully, my happiness over my physical appearance was outweighing my depression regarding how others were treating me. I began to appreciate the deeper aspects of transitioning, like changing your name. I wrote, "I'm so glad that you get to change your name if you want. When you are named by someone else, it doesn't seem *yours*. I feel like I took charge of my own life in naming myself and after all, transitioning is all about taking charge of your own body and mind."

Sarah, my new counselor, kept reinforcing that if someone had an issue with my presentation that it was their issue and not mine. I needed to stop making everyone's problems my own and only accept things that I had control over. Sarah's advice came at a good time considering my divorce was to be final the following month. I was sad to see the marriage end and I cried initially when thinking about it but really, I wasn't married to her. She had married a man, I was miserable trying to be one, and the marriage wouldn't work with me as my true self. I felt a twinge of guilt and wished I had known that I was trans earlier. It is always one of those things people consider and want to ask people. "Would you do it sooner?" "Do you wish…?" I initially wished I would have known sooner but looking back now, I think everything worked out for the best.

CHAPTER 3
Embracing Ella

My zeal for life continued. By now it was a little over a full year of using the proper restroom and I had an experience in the woman's room at school that amused me enough to write about it in my blog. I rarely encountered another female in the school's woman's room because my class was at 5pm and campus was a ghost town. Well, this night I walked into a stall, sat down, and began tinkling. Suddenly, from a few stalls down I hear a, "pfllllllllft!" and a small sigh of relief. I started laughing softly to the point where I farted too. Except, mine was louder... A few stalls over I heard a voice go in a sort of "valley girl" voice, "Oh my Godddddddd."

A week later, I decided I wanted to get a tattoo. Well, I didn't spontaneously decide it, I had the idea rolling around in my head for a while. It was the same tattoo parlor that I gotten my Crawford piercing done at because they had good Google reviews. The tattoo artist was a cool lady. She had this little backpack that reminded me of a chaurus carapace from the Elder Scrolls series. I wanted a semi-colon tattoo incorporated into something pretty. I looked around on Google images and I saw a few pretty tattoos that were butterflies with semi-colons for the body. It was exactly what I wanted!

The tattoo artist printed out some of the ideas I showed her. "What kind of butterfly do you want?" she asked as she was looking over the pictures.

Unfortunately, I wasn't this prepared. I just knew the basic idea of what I wanted. "Honestly, I have no idea," I replied sheepishly, "I just had the basic idea in my head. You're the artist, what do you think would look pretty?" I finished playfully.

The artist smirked, "Well I'm not doing a monarch butterfly. Everyone does monarch butterflies and it's stupid." She grabbed some paper and began drawing. "I want it to have spikes on the lower part of the wing," she explained as she glided her hand across the paper.

"Yeah! That looks cool," I said, "It looks delicate but has a little tough side to it too." The tattoo artist smiled again and grabbed a sheet of tracing paper. Then she grabbed a gel style pen and traced the tattoo design onto the tracing paper.

"Ok, hold out your wrist," she instructed me. I stuck my right wrist out to her despite being left-handed "Do you want it facing out or facing you?" she asked me.

I pondered for a second. "Well I'm getting the tattoo for me and

I want it to remind me of how far I've come. So, facing me please."

She positioned the tracing paper over my wrist with the design facing me and pressed down evenly so that the ink transferred onto my skin. "Ok. Follow me," she said, and I followed her into the tattoo room.

I walked into a room with a big dentist-style chair but with black leather and a side desk to put your arm on. She had me put my right arm onto the tray and began prepping.

"So, like, what's the ink made of?" I asked curiously. I was very calm. After doing bloodwork every three months and getting my face zapped every two weeks, this was cake! Right?

She grabbed some little containers and shook them up and she continued to prepare. "They're all natural. Most of them are made from plants and the ink sits on a layer underneath."

I nodded. I had figured tattoo ink was toxic and would cause cancer the way they tell you in elementary school to not draw on yourself with a ballpoint pen. "So, what about touch-ups?"

"Oh, those will be far off down the road," she answered as she sat down and turned the needle on and off. "Just take care of it when you go out in the sun and you'll be fine." She looked at the vials of color, peeked at the computer, and seemed satisfied with how she had everything. "Now we need some music," she explained, "I can't focus on art without music." She rolled her stool over to the computer and dialed up a music folder.

"What kind of music do you like?" I asked. I figured she wasn't the type of woman who'd be listening to Katy Perry's "Roar" while tattooing, nor Godsmack's "Awake". Clearly, she was not a "mainstream" gal.

"I like trance and electronica," she replied, "This is Boy Harsher. Yeah. Let's do that," she continued to herself and hit "play."

This catchy song with interesting music filled the room.

You see me

you see a stranger

I see you I see danger

Pain, always pain

Pain, always pain

Pain

Breaks rhythm

Breaks rhythm

Breaks rhythm

And repeatedly. I began tilting my head back and forth and repeating the, "pain, breaks rhythm, breaks rhythm, breaks rhythm." The tattoo artist looked up at me and smirked and she continued to tattoo my arm.

THE tattoo took about an hour to complete and I laughed when she was doing certain spots because it tickled! She put some ointment on it and we discussed how to care for it as she wrapped it with plastic wrap.

"Just keep it moist," she explained to me, "I recommend Aquaphor and apply a heavy layer when it feels dry but leave this wrap on for a few hours."

"Yeah, my ex used A&D ointment. You know? The diaper rash stuff." I said matter-of-factly.

She nodded, "Yeah that's ok too. Now. The top layer will peel off the next few days and it's going to be very itchy." She began sounding sterner like a scorning mother. "Do NOT itch it or peel it because you'll ruin it. The skin is just healing itself. You figure, we just sat here for an hour and stabbed underneath it with a fast-moving needle, but you're all set. We can go back to the front desk."

I followed her back out to the front desk where she thought for a second before shooting me a price. I gladly paid with tip and bounded out to my car excited about my "courage" getting a tattoo and just how more outgoing I was. I felt so much happier now that I was more and more my true self.

CHAPTER 5
The Calm Before The Storm

I GOT MY tattoo November 16th, 2017 and I have no significant writings until April 1st, 2018. I was just content with myself, working, and keeping busy with school.

I did end up getting a second tattoo, this time on my left wrist, because I felt the story ended on my right wrist and I needed to show the beginning of the journey. The left wrist was a more original idea inspired from Sylvia Plath's <u>The Bell Jar</u> with a caterpillar crawling up a red rose (Sylvia's favorite flower) while stuck in a bell jar. "I am, I am, I am" is written in a typewriter font underneath the jar which is what Sylvia said to herself when she was discharged from the hospital she was at after her suicide attempt. Unfortunately, I wasn't considering that "Beauty and the Beast" had a rose under a bell jar. So, while I get compliments on the tattoo, they are not necessarily about what it truly symbolizes.

THE main event during this timeframe was that I was now seeking gender affirmation surgery. I felt happy with my transition and still hated my penis. At this point, I was two years into hormone replacement therapy, my name and marker had been changed for a year, and I had been doing electrolysis for over a year. I began noticing everything else coming into focus on my body. The thinning of facial hair and softer face was causing me less anxiety when going out in public, I was growing my hair out, and my B-cup breasts were validating to my identity.

As a result, it became more and more magnified that my penis was still there, and I hated it the more female I looked. I needed another surgery recommendation before I could get anything started and so I looked up the Center for Psychosexual Health and began meetings there.

I felt very frustrated when I left my intake meeting at CPH. Not only was it seventy-five bucks because they don't take insurance, but I felt exposed and humiliated at the hands of a new "therapist". I put therapist in quotes because I feel that CPH is more of a transgender "gatekeeper" than an actual place of caring and helping.

The counselor asked me a ton of questions to gauge how dysphoric I was. When did I know? How did I know? What behaviors did I exhibit early on? I mentioned the laundry incidents I experienced as a pre-teen which prompted further probing from the therapist.

"Well, what was it about the underwear that you enjoyed the

most?" She asked with a notebook open as she waited to write.

I thought for a minute or two, "I would say the texture," I began, "I have a bunch of old Chatham blankets that I bought, you know? The acrylic ones that have the satin trim? They remind me of that."

She scribbled into the notebook, "So you liked the feel of them?" She wrote some more, "What about patterns?"

I flinched a little and tensed up as I thought. "I guess I would say I liked the leopard print. Stuff like that" I closed my eyes in embarrassment.

The counselor chuckled and continued to smile as she wrote. "So, you liked the racy stuff?" She continued with a hint of teasing in her voice.

I felt myself blushing, "Yeah, I guess so," I answered quietly.

"Well what about later in life?" She asked, "Did you engage in this behavior? Did you wear woman's clothing?"

I started getting angry and raised my voice, "Yeah, I cross-dressed in college but then I stopped because my professor humiliated me in front of the class."

The counselor looked down at her notes. "Yes, you did mention that. So, you enjoyed wearing woman's clothes?"

Finally, I snapped. I was having a hard time realizing how any of this probing was relevant. What was this bullshit? The Spanish Inquisition? (No one expects the Spanish Inquisition). It was hard enough paying half a day's worth of work and now I was taking this grilling from a stranger. I looked up sternly into her eyes which is something I still have difficulty doing when I interact with others.

"Look, I have been transitioning for over two years. I have been living as a female for at least a year now when my name and marker were official. The depression from dealing with this caused me to lose a good job. I'm in the middle of getting divorced. My family disowned me. I am NOT doing this for fun," I finished vehemently as I was practically yelling at the end.

She seemed taken aback by this response and complimented me for having progressed this far into transitioning with little to no guidance. Then she proceeded to bash my gynecologist for allowing me to take hormone replacement therapy without assessing me.

"What assessments did your doctor do with you to determine that you have gender dysphoria?" she asked rather haughtily.

I frowned, "She didn't do any. I was already ordering hormone therapy from online and had been taking them for four months before I even went to her."

"Well that's not acceptable," she retorted as she wrote in her notebook. "How did you even hear about her then?"

I cut in, "From the Pride Center," I snapped back. "I thought I already let you know all of this. She works on 'informed consent' so as long as you understand the medication risks, you can start provided you do the proper follow-ups."

"So, she hasn't done any assessments with you at all?" She retorted as she feverously wrote.

"No," I answered bitterly. I began feeling that obtaining my second letter was going to be a goat-hike of epic proportion. I really needed to start all over? Who was this bitch to chastise how I was transitioning? She had said multiple times during this session that

I passed very well and that she was impressed with how I presented myself. So why was she trying to piss me off? A test?

She sensed my anxiety and she softened her demeanor. "Look," she began quietly, "I'm just here to help you. I commend you again for doing this all on your own. I just wish you would have come here first."

I rolled my eyes and sighed.

"Who does your bloodwork?" she asked gently.

"My doctor writes me a prescription and I take it to Quest Diagnostics," I answered with my guard coming down a bit.

"See?" she started and nodded to the room next door, "we have an endocrinologist on site." She scribbled more in the notebook.

I felt tears welling up in my eyes and I started to cry. "Whatever then. That's why I'm here, I guess. To try and get on track. It's not like I *knew* what to do!" I started bawling.

"Well let's do that then, let's get you on track," she said. "I want to see you in two weeks. Come on," she finished and got out of her chair and opened her door.

I followed her out while wiping my eyes and made another appointment at the desk with the receptionist.

CHAPTER 6
The Gatekeeper Games

I DROVE TO the Pride Center to see if Cameron was there after my grueling session. I reflected with him on the session and how the counselor made me feel like a glorified cross-dresser. I wanted the surgery and was beginning to like myself. We talked for about an hour and I felt better afterwards. That night I wrote:

> "I still have more electrolysis to do and to work on voice, walk, mannerisms more but it's coming along. I have to say that I am a lot more confident and comfortable with myself now that I have gotten over the bumps. I am blossoming into quite an attractive woman."

So why was this counselor making it so hard?

I had session again at CPH on April 17th, 2018 and it continued my foul mood about the place. This time, I spent seventy-five dollars to sit in a library to do a poorly worded Scantron test (I mean assessment…) regarding my mental health. I only got to talk with the "therapist" for about ten minutes after that and I concluded that she was a short stumpy troll with a condescending attitude. I felt belittled that I didn't ask <u>her</u> for permission to start hormones.

In my experience, these cis-het therapists and doctors we interact with always like to tell us how many years of gender studies they have or how many books and journal articles they've written on gender, but they still do <u>not</u> truly <u>know</u> shit about what <u>we</u> go through. While I understand that it is difficult to empathize to something you have never experienced firsthand, a good doctor, therapist, or friend, at least will <u>listen</u> and not sit there judging and making you feel like a piece of shit. After all, it was <u>my</u> decision to start HRT and to change my name and marker. I am clearly happier with <u>my</u> body and <u>my</u> life. So, isn't that enough for her? Why should I feel helpless and controlled by some person I didn't even know until two weeks ago? My interactions with her briefly made me consider just living my life and not seeking GAS. Perhaps that's what her intentions were.

I simmered down that night and vowed that I would play the "gatekeeper games" because I <u>wanted</u> the surgery. My boyfriend stated that this counselor was testing me to see if I had resolve to pursue it. I noticed something interesting about my body the following morning when I was getting dressed that eased the rest of my insecurity.

"Hey hun," I yelled from my bedroom, "can you come here for a second please?"

"Huh? What is it," my boyfriend's groggy voice emanated from his room.

"I don't know. Maybe this bra just needs to be adjusted or something. My boobs don't seem to be fitting in them right," I said, trying to adjust my straps and trying to lift my boobs so that they would fit better into the cups.

I heard the half-asleep "slip-slide" of feet across his room into mine.

"Hum, it looks okay to me," he answered sleepily.

"No," I said firmly, "something's messed up. They're not fitting in there right. Do you see?" I asked frustrated.

My boyfriend looked at my chest and at the straps. "Well I have no idea. It's not like *I* wear them or anything," he responded humorously.

I sighed and rolled my eyes. "Well maybe it's time to get fitted. I haven't been fitted for a bra before and have been thinking about doing it. You figure I've had boobs for a year and a half now."

He shrugged and rubbed his eyes. "Yeah. It can't hurt. Do it up. Who does them anyway?"

I looked down at my chest and ill-fitting brassiere. "I remember seeing that Aerie or Victoria's Secret does fittings. I guess I'll go to Aerie. I think Vic's Secret would be too intimidating."

He nodded. "Yeah. I would go and see."

Later that afternoon, I went to Aerie at the local mall. I felt confident as I strutted through the mall but then I got anxious as I walked into the store's door. It wasn't a sense of dread as it was a sense of being overwhelmed. I felt like I finally belonged at a woman's store like this and didn't want to make a fool of myself with my excitement.

"Can I help you," this cute twenty-something manning (womaning) the front counter said to me.

"Umm," I began softly so only she could hear, "I read that you guys do free fittings."

She smiled, hopefully not wondering why I was being so bashful, "Yeah we do. Would you like for me to do it here or in the dressing room?"

"In there," I answered while meekly pointing to the dressing room. She grabbed a measuring tape from a drawer and slung it over her shoulders.

"Okay. Follow me." I followed her into the dressing room. "What kind of bra are you wearing today?" She asked while taking the measuring tape off her shoulders.

"Umm," I began, "it's just a basic push-up bra." I couldn't believe this. I was in a woman's dressing room getting bra fitted! It may sound so dumb on how nervous I was but be fair here. This was a huge milestone.

"Okay," she answered as she measured across my torso and then outwards, "how much padding do you like?"

I blushed a little, "not too much padding. I don't want like Dolly Parton boobs or anything," I finished with some confidence.

She smiled and placed her measuring tape back onto her shoulders. "Well according to this, you are a 36D," she said.

My jaw dropped to the floor. "No way!" I said flabbergasted and snapped my bra straps under my sweater, "this is a B."

The clerk nodded sympathetically, "Well, what sorts of problems are you having with your current fit?" she asked.

Any sort of embarrassment I felt earlier was now gone. Here we were, two women talking about bra fitting in the dressing room where, by the way, a mother was waiting for her teenage daughter. "They just don't fit. Like I feel I am spilling out of the thing."

She nodded again, "well, around eighty percent of women are wearing the wrong bra. Let me grab you a few in that 36D."

"Let's try a C," I said stupidly. "I just can't believe I'm a D." The lady smiled and didn't seem angry with my ignorance.

"Okay," she answered as she unlocked a dressing room door, "you go get ready in there and I'll bring you back one. We can try the D after you see what you think."

I entered the dressing room with mirrors on all corners and began reading the post-it notes with nice body-positive statements written on them, and I heard her footsteps get more faint. I wish I still had the picture in my phone but one of the post-it notes caught my eye almost immediately. I got teary-eyed when I read it and felt okay being there. It said something like "Respect. Trans-women are women here."

"Here you go," the woman said draping a bra over the dressing room door, "try that on and see how it fits."

"Thanks," I replied and began trying the bra on. I got the straps comfortable and investigated my reflection in the mirrors and swiveled around a bit with excitement.

"What do you think?" the lady's voice asked nicely from the other side of the door.

"Umm, I'm not sure," I answered dumbly and looking at the cups over my chest, "I think it's too small."

I could sense the clerk's glee that she knew she was right in telling me I was a D. "Okay, give me that one back and we'll try the D." So, I handed her the bra over the door and heard her walk back into the store.

I stood topless admiring my breasts in the mirrors for a few minutes before I heard bra buckles click off the top of the door yet again.

"Here's the D," she said, "I'll be right back to check on you." I looked at the cups of the bra and turned it over in my hands. The things seemed huge! I looked down at my chest. There was no way! But she was clearly the expert, not me, and so I clasped the bra, spun it around, and began slipping my arms through. They seemed to fit correctly into the cups, but I had too much slack on the straps and was trying to finagle the little buckles to make them tighter. There. I think it fit ok.

"How's it going in there hun," the clerk's voice returned.

"Could you come in here?" I asked, "I just want your opinion."

"Sure. Open up," she answered, and I cracked the door and stood in the corner, so no one would see my topless body. She looked me up and down for a second and then at my bra fitting job. "Here, let me just check you," she said as she began adjusting my straps, "how do the cups fit?"

"Well they fit in there really well," I answered happily, "I think I just don't have the straps right."

She continued to buzz around my back and gently cinching the little buckles on the straps. "Yeah, you'd be surprised at how a little adjusting can make a bra feel amazing. I really like our bras here. I can wear mine all day and not even notice. It's a bad addiction working in a store like this," she finished with a giggle.

"I bet," I replied, "and wow that feels and looks really good. Thank you soooo much. I feel so much better now."

I put my right hand on my hip and swiveled back and forth and she looked at my reflection in the mirror as my smile beamed. "So, everything is good then? I picked you out a push-up with the lightest padding. Meet me back on the floor and I'll show you where they are." I nodded, and she left so that I could don my old too-tight bra and sweater. I met her back on the floor and she showed me some options. "What colors do you want?" She asked.

"Ugh. Well I'm color-blind. What about blue, red, and black. Every woman needs a black bra," I said reciting some sexual dogma. She rifled through the drawers and picked me out the colors.

"What do you think?" She asked holding three different colors in her hands.

I scanned the selection, "That's perfect," I concluded. I also ended up getting a few pair of boy shorts and some other undies and I like how Aerie doesn't call them "panties". The woman said that it makes them sound dirty and that Aerie is about loving yourself as a woman. They have their AerieREAL campaign which really embraces woman's positivity, and I'm so glad that I went there. I felt hugged by a chic feminine vibe. I felt confident to be a woman instead of vulnerable and that's coming from me who had only been living as one for a year and a half.

All in all, I spent $150. Well actually the total was like $260 but I opened an Aerie card and had sale prices with that. I profusely thanked the woman for all of her help and left the store with my head held high with proper fitting and cute bras.

CHAPTER 7
Ella Goes Atomic

MY BOYFRIEND AND I had a day off together (an oddity with my whack-a-doo work schedule) and I was scrolling through the movies available on Netflix. I was in the "A" section and saw that "Atomic Blonde" was an available movie to watch. I had always wanted to watch the movie because I liked the main character's blonde hair and style. I also sort of feel badass like her character.

Not to delve too much into the movie itself because it wasn't that good to begin with but it's about the "atomic blonde" working as a spy against the Russians (how original right?). The movie begins at the end of her mission with her sitting in a sort of interrogation room while Rosanne Barr's husband or you may know him as the crazy vet from "The Big Lebowski" is trying to discern what the heck happened on her mission.

Flashback to her mission and you get a bunch of action scenes with a "Jason Bourne" plot of some guy trying to do something bad, and kill her while doing it. I began to get bored with the movie and was eye-rolling at her fight scenes since the lead actress was kicking these guy's asses while probably weighing like 130 pounds soaking wet.

Jealousy began to increasingly set in as I became fixated on the woman's body and the pretty/cute/sexy outfits that she wore. There was even a lesbian scene and I began questioning my sexuality and yearning to be with a woman. I started looking for a pair of knee-high boots in the style like hers. I looked on numerous shoe store websites but the lack of options in my size led me to become depressed. Self-loathing kicked in and I hated everything about transitioning. I would never be a "real" woman like her. I had facial hair, I felt fat since I was probably 30 pounds heavier, I didn't walk sexy like her, my feet are too big, and I had a penis. All I had was her hair color, her haircut, and boobs.

I decided to cull this negative self-talk by walking to the convenience store down the street for a snack and Snapple. I asked James if he had some headphones and plugged them into my phone and began blasting my "Savior" by Rise Against channel off Pandora. I walked very briskly with anger as I mouthed the words to the various songs the Pandora algorithm felt I would like. Artists like "Linkin Park", "3 Days Grace", "Disturbed", "Staind", and more "Rise Against" filled my head. Looking back, I know it made me more upset about my thoughts. While I was walking back, "The Cranberries" song "Zombie" played followed by the "Bad Wolves" version and it pushed me over the edge.

I walked back inside the house where James was still watching the movie and gave him his earbuds back in silence. I then proceeded to go up to my room, closed the door, and began blasting Pandora from my Amazon Echo Dot. I started crying on my bed and began looking at the knife I had on my desk. I didn't want to do it. No. Don't do it. I had been doing so well.

My mind kept telling me to just calm down, but I couldn't resist. I grabbed the knife and began slicing across my upper arm. It left thin cuts that gently bled before clotting in the air with red burn marks afterwards. It felt good to me and eased my mental anguish. James came upstairs at the end of the movie and opened the door to my room. I felt disconnected from reality and looked at him as if he were a ghost. He asked me what was wrong, and I just stared at him and pointed to the knife laying on my blanket. He looked at the knife, then at me aghast, and asked me where I self-harmed. I pointed to my upper arm and he instructed me go to the bathroom, so he could clean it up. The peroxide hurt like hell and he stuck a square gauze bandage over the burning, thinly cut skin. It had been the first time in seemingly forever that I self-harmed and I felt like I betrayed myself since I had the semi-colon tattoo.

I went to sleep in my bedroom for the rest of the night feeling depressed and ashamed.

Please try to call someone, anyone, if you ever feel like hurting yourself. Even if it's the tenth person on your safety plan, please try to do something other than hurting yourself. I know it can feel hopeless. I have borderline personality disorder with PTSD. So, I know how helpless you can feel. It's not necessarily your fault that you feel this way. You are not "sick", and you are not a victim of an "illness." The chain can be broken. Please take care of yourself.

Call your counseling office. Mine has afterhours staff. Yours may also. 1-800-273-8255 is the national suicide prevention line. 877-565-8860 is the trans lifeline. Please stay alive. Tomorrow is a new day.

CHAPTER 8
Growth And Change

FINAL EXAMS SOON were upon me and I was becoming exhausted between staying up late after work to finish up the semester. I noticed my body more as far as my softer face and my puffed-out breasts. Even my counselor Sarah said that I was doing a lot better with my confidence.

My self-assurance was causing me to change my stances on ideologies that I developed from my Instagram addiction which I eventually broke by deleting my account. "Passing" is a concept that agitates me along with the idea that being "stealth" is some disservice to the trans community. To "pass" means that you physical appear as your gender/sex and your interactions allow you to be such. I hate this term because to me it implies that you are wearing a sheep's clothing, that you are playing a role in a movie, or that every day that you go out in public you are taking a test.

The Yang & Yin of Gender Transiton

Talk about anxiety-ridden! I sometimes get anxious going out and I think I "pass" perfectly. We don't need to look at it that way and compound the stress of being transgender.

Being "stealth" goes hand-in-hand with "passing". With stealth, you do not discuss your trans status, typically avoid the community, and have no identifiers with your trans status. What's so wrong with that!? To me, the whole point of transitioning is to live your life as close as you can to your "cis" counterparts. I do not see how constantly wearing your trans status allows you to move pass transitioning. We are more than that identification.

How can you enjoy being your true self if you are constantly hung up on it?

I have a trans pride flag in my room and my tattoos reflect my gender/sex transition and my growth living with my mental health. I have no shame being trans and I do not mind discussing it when asked in a respectful manner. It just rarely comes up now with the way I look and act. I prefer it this way! On the flip side, I should not be shamed by other trans people for keeping it to myself. I just don't need to shout it from the rooftops and a lot of the "oh, you're a sell-out" or "oh, you're ashamed" come from people who enjoy being an "outcast" or who are jealous. All in all, the people who transition to purposely stick out or who over embrace being trans should not be transitioning. It's obviously a fine line since you cannot fully understand a person's mental health, but I've interacted with trans people who have trans tattoos and wear female clothes yet act, look and sound like men. Maybe they're non-binary or genderqueer or whatever and whatever to them. It just muddies the waters for us binary folk who want acceptance.

My trans flag and tattoos are a symbol of pride but it is for me. It is a pride in myself for persevering and a pride in our community for battling for equality. I am currently fighting my health insurance company for equal benefits. (1/31/19) Even though I live in New York State, my company's health insurance is excluding trans care. That is the kind of pride I want to believe in. I see that flag as a symbol of inner peace. When I go to bed at night and look up at my flag or when I wake up in the morning and look up, I feel a calmness envelop me. I suppose it's whatever the beholder wants to feel.

CHAPTER 9
Ella Writes a Note

The oscillations in my relationship with my boyfriend, the acceptance to self-doubt, and thoughts and dreams about Christina caught up to me one night. With my boyfriend, we'd be ok for a while, do something fun, and then go for long stretches with no intimacy or a relationship at all. The loneliness and feelings of abandonment made me upset, and there were plenty of stretches where I would cry myself to sleep in my room wondering what I was doing wrong. When I wasn't crying, I would lay in bed and reflect on my past relationship with Christina and think about the time we shared together.

It finally caught up to me at 4 AM on 6/14/2018. I woke up after having a dream about Christina. In the dream, I was having a breakdown at our old house and she called for an ambulance. The ambulance came, the paramedics strapped me to a bed, and took me to the psychiatric hospital where I lived in a room by myself. I woke up crying and wanted to die. I spent the day at work thinking about what people in my life would say about me when I was gone. I wrote my goodbye note on my lunch break at work. In the note, I apologized to my parents and James for what I was planning, I gave my possessions to James, and even stated that I wanted to be buried in my black and yellow Polka-dot dress and to do my makeup and hair.

I called my counselor about my feelings and read the note to her. She informed me that my statement needed to be taken very seriously and that I would need to come in to see her after work. I finished off the day and drove to her office. I waited for about an hour for her return to her office. She informed me that there was a bed for me at a hospital.

I began crying and nodded to her because I knew that I needed to go. Unfortunately, when she went back out to talk to my psychologist, my insurance wasn't accepted there. Plan B was to call her when I got home from work every night to check-in or use the after-hours line who lets the counselors know.

I followed through with Plan B for the week and began to feel better afterwards. Perhaps I just needed a little outside support since I wasn't getting any at home. I needed to learn to stand on my own two feet and to self-care. I am a lot stronger now and can better help myself.

CHAPTER 10
He's Trying

My father's birthday was coming up on August 15th and I decided to go out on a limb and send him a card for his birthday. I walked over to the Walgreens next to work and bought a fifty-dollar Olive Garden gift card. My intent was that mom and dad could go out to dinner and at least save them some hassle.

I attempted to again contact him via email. Our last correspondence five months prior did not start well as I was called a "fucking little selfish prick", I was told to go "fuck myself", and that my ways were "fucked up". Regardless if he didn't agree with my decision it was absolutely disgusting to swear and say those things to your own child. Yet I'm "fucked up". My only salvo was that his responses were "hilarious coming from an abuser."

Things went silent until I wrote him an email with his birthday coming up:

> *There is a birthday card with a gift card coming. Please don't just throw it out.*

Surprisingly, he wrote something back:

> *I wouldn't just throw it out. Thank you for being so thoughtful. I hope all is well with you. Even though I don't agree with the life choices you've decided to make, you're still my flesh and blood. And there isn't anything that can change that. I've also come to the realization that no matter what I say &/or whatever opinions I have about what you're doing, none of it's going to change anything. Still, this doesn't mean I'm in total acceptance. I'm still struggling with the reality of it. Someday I hope to fully come to terms with it, but I'm not quite there yet.*
>
> *All in all, I hope that you're happy and healthy. I never want to hear that you've tried to commit suicide again. That's the worst thing any parent ever wants to hear. Please don't ever try that again. I'd be so devastated. Knowing that I somehow could've helped, been a better father, better person, would be too much guilt for me to handle...*
>
> *Well, I'd better get back to work. I have a lot to do, in a very short time (what else is new). Take care and be safe.*
>
> *With love,*
> *Dad*

I cried at work when I received the email. I showed my manager. I showed my co-workers. I felt that perhaps he could redeem himself and we could start over. I'm still waiting for that time to come but that last reply is better than the predecessor. For sure.

CHAPTER 11
This Is How We Do It

SEPTEMBER AND OCTOBER were just everyday months. I had my GRS consult with Dr. Burke at the end of November. My head was spinning afterwards, and I was having a hard time recognizing why I felt conflicted and almost sad about it.

After the typical check-in (insurance card, address, pharmacy, etc.), I met with a nurse who did the usual vitals and asked a myriad of questions regarding my medical history. I stated at the end that I am healthy as a horse and chuckled to try and calm down. Then she asked me why I was seeing Dr. Burke. I felt uncomfortable answering that I was there for a vaginoplasty and I started to feel depressed. I'm not in denial about being transsexual, but I think having to admit that I am to cis women makes me feel insecure and inferior. Like I'm fake/pretending or less of a woman. I feel exposed when talking about it because I know they are judging me. As a result, the consultation was difficult to focus on.

Once we were done with vitals and my admission of why I was there, I was led into a huge room with a doctor bed with a huge dentist style light over it, some chairs, and the obligatory sink with Purell. This other woman came in with a clipboard, sat down in one of the chairs across from my chair and proceeded to ask me questions. I don't even think she gave me her name. Again, the first question was regarding why I was there.

"I'm here to discuss bottom surgery," I said quietly and choosing my words deliberately. She jotted it down on her clipboard and then ANOTHER woman came in (again I can't remember her telling me her name) and AGAIN asked me why I was here. Saying gender reassignment surgery again to another woman made me feel more inferior. It was deflating my morale and self-confidence. I'm sitting in a room with a woman in a chair and a woman standing off to my side answering that I'm here about getting a surgery I need to feel complete. A surgery to change my penis into a vagina.

Knowing that I have a penis already bothers me a lot when I'm alone getting dressed, going to the bathroom, or showering because I feel that I look incredibly attractive up until that point (no pun intended). I'm sure they deal with trans women on a consistent basis and it probably doesn't bother them or else they wouldn't be working with a surgeon who does the surgery. However, being around other women and admitting that I'm trans hurts me emotionally. Like I don't really belong.

The lady looked at me and so I rephrased my answer from "gender reassignment surgery."

"GRS", I answered hesitantly. Then I just shook my head with frustration and blurted out, "a vaginoplasty."

"Ok. Any electrolysis?" She asked.

"Um yes," I started anxiously. I felt like I was in an inquisition or some sort of oral exam. I shook my head to get the buzzing out of my ears. My vision started to blur. Damn why was it so bright in this room? "I mean up here, not down there," I finished quickly and pointing to my face.

"Ok," she responded as she scribbled, "Any prior surgeries?"

"No," I answered confidently. Finally, an easy question!

"So, no top surgery?" She asked.

"Hell no," I answered, "They're fine," I finished cocky. (pun intended). Then I glanced at the lady's chest. She was maybe 5'9" 130 and an A cup if she was lucky. Not to sound like a bitch, but that mental comparison was something I needed. At this point, anything would have worked to make me feel less insecure and more authentic.

"Ok, we're all set and now I'll go get Dr. Burke," she finished up and left the room.

Dr. Burke came in, introduced himself, grabbed a white board marker, and quickly sketched two thighs split open sitting on its buttocks with a floppy penis pointed up at the 3 o'clock position. It was like something out of a drawing party game. It was worthy of an art gallery. That's what 10 years of medical school lets you accomplish ladies and gentlemen. Surprisingly the picture on the whiteboard didn't bother me. I was too numb. My eyes couldn't focus. I was in a haze and why was it so damn bright in this room!? What bothered me was that there were 3 other women in the room with me now. The first woman I knew for 10 minutes, the other one 5 minutes, and the last one had just walked in with Dr. Burke. So, I had never seen her before. It was very overwhelming, and I felt exposed even though I was still in my street clothes.

Dr. Burke explained the procedure at length while I sat in my fog and nodded my head. I already knew all about the procedure and what to expect. At the end, he explained that I could call for a follow-up once I was nicotine free for a month. I was not a heavy smoker (five to ten daily) and I was very excited that I was so close. I just told myself that it is what it is, and I just needed to get over it. These people were here to help, but I don't know, I just felt like a freak, incomplete, and embarrassed...

CHAPTER 12
A Machine Gun Of Events

FROM DECEMBER 2018 to April 2019, I have spent the last four months knowing only fine automotive work and breathing. At lot has happened recently so let's get right to it.

I received my New York State inspector's license at the end of December 2018. We transferred a tire tech to a different store, fired our only other inspector, and another tire tech got another job. We have been working extremely shorthanded. Thankfully, we sniped a tech from another store and have two new guys starting; one of them is cute and has an inspector's license. For the past few months, I have been doing the work of at least two people. I even bought a tool cabinet that I decorated with 8x8 pictures of Madonna, Cindy Lauper, and Sylvia Plath. The final square on my box is up for grabs. I have my own lightweight yet powerful air impact gun which ironically is a Craftsman, my own socket sizes we constantly use, a screwdriver set, a plier set, my Craftsman mechanics set, and other small useful items. So yeah, I have been extremely busy with work.

I began feeling what I described to a few friends as being apathetic. I looked down at my "Ella, asst. mngr." patch on my work shirt and felt detached from who I was. I didn't feel "Ella". I didn't know who "Ella" was, but I wanted her to come back to me. It was a very weird experience like I was observing this woman buzz around working and yearning to be her.

I looked in the mirror again constantly before this out of body existence and would see a woman I didn't recognize. I was a stranger to myself! I wrote about this in my blog:

...I feel detached from her. A prisoner locked away in a transcendent Bastille.

I see my flats, heels, and sneakers on the shoe rack and it appears like a shoe store. Lonely shoes looking for someone who fits them proper.

I don my bra at dawn, gazing at an unfamiliar body, constantly morphing at its own will. 185, 142, 160, 162, 155, 34A, 36B, 36D. She is constantly shifting like a child pushing vegetables around their plate.

That is transitioning. A journey with no map through the mind and body.

I am happy. I feel peaceful. I am not afraid or conflicted about my decision. I suppose I must become reacquainted with this woman. This "Ella" who is beckoning with rouge

*lips and roguish smirk. I knew her a few months ago.
I will know her again.*

I LAID DOWN in bed after posting, but I couldn't get my mind to relax. I just felt lost and hopeless. My mind kept racing that transitioning was stupid. That I was ugly. That I would never really be a woman and was just playing pretend and that I would never get my GRS.

I began thinking of self-harming as a distraction, to feel anything other than this emptiness, but I knew that committing self-harm may set me back on my treatment and surgery. I hadn't cut since a year ago and I was doing fine. I was running my errands. I was getting gendered correctly nearly all the time. I felt confident in going out instead of scared/anxious like before. I was making good money at work. So, what the heck happened? Was it burnout from work? Was it that I was in a holding pattern for my surgery? Boredom or borderline tendency to self-sabotage when one's life is stable. At times I have felt that I perform better under pressure and thrive in chaos even if I appear too pressured.

Regardless the reason, the thought didn't go away even though I tried to relax and will it away. I sharpened the knife I used before and began slashing away at my upper thigh to try and feel something. It was bad, but I am not trying to glorify it or sound proud of the damage I did. I will have scars and the thought of that is frustrating alone since I was doing so well. Counseling the next day helped.

Please do not hurt yourself. Do not beat yourself up though if you cannot resist the urge to hurt yourself. Think about all the times that you did not self-harm. Think about the times you used your skills or talked to someone about what was troubling you. We all make mistakes. It will get better.

THINGS got a whole lot better the day after counseling! Had I just have held on like Wilson Philips for one more day I would have been uplifted. I received an email from Transcend Legal who had been working with my insurance company and Mavis to lift the transgender exclusion that Mavis put on our health plan. The email states that the exclusion has been lifted and signed off by Mavis!

From my health insurance:
> Language has been added regarding Gender Dysphoria in accordance with the requirements of Section 1557 of the Affordable Care Act (ACA) as it pertains to covered entities.
> Under mental health exclusions, language stating "Changes incurred for treatment of sexual dysfunction (other than organic causes) or any procedure associated with a sex change operation" has been removed.
> Revised Gender Transition reference.
> A definition of Gender Dysphoria has been added.
> Under Totally Disabled: language stating "Changes incurred for treatment of sexual dysfunction (other than organic causes) or any procedure associated with a sex

change operation" has been removed.

Signed: some squiggly from Mavis.

Talk about change! Talk about making a difference! Mavis LLC has 3,000 employees according to the North American Industry Classification System (NAICS). NAICS is the standard used by Federal statistical agencies in classifying business establishments for collecting, analyzing, and publishing statistical data related to the U.S. business economy. Mavis has a sales volume of $2.5 billion dollars. I sincerely hope that they weren't riding Trump's argument saying that it would cost them too much money to cover transgender care. Transgender people make up only 0.5-0.6% of the population. So, if you say that Mavis follows these statistics, Mavis has 150 transgender employees. I'm sure with $2.5 billion dollars they will survive. I'd love to meet any other trans employees we have. I didn't just want this for myself.

CHAPTER 13
Ella Can See Clearly Now The Blur Is Gone

I AM WRITING this chapter wearing my pink Oakley sunglasses since I do not want eye strain while typing. Granted my monitor is a 1080p 32" television that sits across the top shelf of my desk but still, no risks. Why am I wearing sunglasses inside you ask? Well today is the day after my Lasik procedure (don't call it surgery). It was probably the best decision that I have ever made, and I consider it my FFS (facial feminization surgery) (don't call it surgery!) because it has really changed how I look. I look more like a woman without my glasses. You can see where my face fat has filled in my face. My nose doesn't seem so prominent to me. My baby blue eyes are vibrant and beckoning to be stared into like a still ocean teeming with life and vibrance. It is so surreal that at first, I was worried I was going to wake up from a dream.

I believe I have worn glasses since I was 17 but I know for a darn fact that I've needed them earlier. I totally recommend America's Best for glasses. They have amped up their selection and quality since I first went 16 years ago. I remember my first time there. The optician literally pulled out a tray from a drawer with like 6 frame options. It was awful. I still think I have my first pair kicking around in the basement on my CD rack. They are grey wire frames with tear drop lenses. America's Best has improved rapidly, and I picked out a pair of Kate Spade frames one of the times afterwards. My mother was annoyed that I was searching in the woman's section of frames.

"That's the woman's section, you goof," she said to me.

"Yeah, I know," I replied as I scanned the selection, "I just feel that I have a small face and that a woman's frame would fit me better. I came across the Kate Spade frames and had to have them. I knew who she was back then because my mother had some of her purses.

I used to go to Lenscrafters after that when I had my own vision coverage, but they are owned by Luxottica which is a giant eyewear monopoly and is part of the reason why they are like $300 for one pair. ("Adam Ruins Everything" with Adam Conover.) My current employer doesn't offer a vision plan, so it was back to someplace inexpensive. America's Best it was, and at my last visit in August 2018 I paid $320 for 2 pairs of Cosmopolitan frames and they used an old frame to make me prescription sunglasses.

Back to the present. It was time to say goodbye to glasses. I went to Dr. Atwal here in Buffalo since my boyfriend had PRK done by him and still has amazing vision at 38 years old. My consultation was a week prior to the procedure. They do another full eye exam because they want the most recent health and prescription of your eyes. I could see 20/15 with glasses so I qualified for blade-free Lasik. The entire staff was wonderful. They are very informative about aftercare regarding the eye drops you will need to use.

I had to watch a 15-minute video after the thorough eye exam regarding the procedure that was probably taped in the late 90's judging by the clothes. The doctor then gave me a 4-page packet of more detailed information and a consent form before having me step back into the exam room for a final conversation.

"So just read over that packet and when you are ready to make a decision, give us a call," the lady said as she pointed to the packet.

"Oh, I have already made my decision," I said bubbly as I nearly was jumping around the room.

The lady shifted back quickly in her chair shocked as if I told her she won the lottery. "Well great! When would you like to schedule? We do the procedures on Thursday"

This worked perfectly for me because I have Thursdays off! "As soon as possible!" I answered giggling.

"OK great! I'll set you up next week on the 9th. I have a 2:30 slot open, does that work for you?" she asked glancing from her computer monitor with colored boxes and back to me.

"I'll take it," I nodded and adding it into my phone, "I am so excited about this."

The lady smiled, "Well that's great to hear. We're all set and if you have any questions, don't hesitate to call us and please make sure you read that packet over and have it ready the day of the procedure."

I bounded out of the office out to my car smiling from ear to ear.

I was extremely amped up the day of my procedure. There were chairs facing a large window as if the waiting room was a movie theater. Oh no! People were going to be watching me while I had this done? Oh God. I was already nervous. The lady at the desk was very nice though, and asked me if I wanted the windows clear or blacked out.

"Closed please," I answered in my best "Ella voice". I felt like I had a hint of "bitchiness" in my voice, but I was already nervous and doing this for myself. I wasn't a zoo exhibit!

"OK, follow me and I'm going to take your blood pressure," the lady said, and I followed her to a chair in a little corner.

"It's probably going to be a jillion," I chuckled as I shifted around in the chair. The lady was trying to Velcro the blood pressure cuff on, but I was still squirmy. "Over a jillion and one," I finished nervously.

"Would you like a valium?" she asked gently as I looked at my feet.

"I thought we were going to do that anyway?" I whispered quickly.

"Well it's certainly a suggestion," the woman said, "I think you need it. It will definitely help you."

She opened the door behind me and came back with two little clear cups. One cup had a small green circle in it and the other was filled halfway with water.

"OK, I want you to chew this and make sure you get all of it with the water. Chewing it makes it work quicker," she instructed as she handed me the cups.

I chewed up the green tablet which didn't taste like anything and washed the sandy particles down with the water. The lady led me into the room where I watched the video during my consultation. She handed me a hair net and instructed me to make sure my hair was all tucked into it. She left after checking my care bag on the desk. I laid on the fluffy couch and flipped through a Home and Garden Magazine to pass the time. The valium was kicking in and I began laughing to myself at the $50 wicker patio chairs and other overpriced items. Then I crashed. I was practically falling asleep and was snoring at one point. I had to stagger out of the room when they came to get me, and I was slightly embarrassed.

I was still loopy when I went into the Lasik room.

"Are you all ready for surgery," the woman asked.

"Don't call it surgery," I said as firmly and humorously as I could through the effects of the valium.

"I'm sorry. Are you ready for the procedure?" she asked with emphasis on the "P" and chuckling.

Dr. Atwal introduced himself and shook my hand. He was super handsome and youthful looking.

He had beautiful brown eyes, an amazing boyish smile, and a neatly trimmed beard.

"OK, Joella. Lay down on the bed hon," he instructed me."

I stared confused at the bed and then noticed the donut looking pillow at the "head" of it. "My head goes there, right?" I said goofily.

"Yep. Just lay there," Dr. Atwal said as he adjusted my head into the donut. "Lift your chin up a hair…good. Just like that," he said. "Do you see the blinking light above you?"

I looked up and noticed the blinking light. "Yea. I see it," I said through my haze.

"Good. Keep looking at the blinking light," he replied as he hovered off to my right side. "Keep looking," he said as the blinking light descended onto my face.

"I'm still looking at it," I said sheepishly as the light seemed a millimeter from my face.

"Good," he answered with a smile, "you're doing good," he finished as he gently opened my right eye with his fingers.

Then this cylinder came down and held my eye open. It was uncomfortable and felt like someone was crushing my eye socket. I felt a gentle squeeze on my shoulder and my hand being held.

"You're doing great Joella. Just breathe and relax," a lady's voice said to my left.

I felt like I was in a "giving birth" scene. Her holding me and hearing my name was so beautiful. All that disassociation from a chapter ago disappeared. I tried to control my breathing.

Then this white light scanned across my eye left to right and then right to left with a whirring sound the same way you see a scanner do on a printer. I smelled a light burning smell that panicked me a little and I groaned in confusion. The blinking light blurred and moved around my field of vision.

"You're doing great hon, just keep breathing," the gentle voice to my left said as she continued to hold my hand and shoulder. My breath was erratic as I tried to stay calm.

"I'm still looking at the blinking light, but I can't see!" I said distressed.

"Good. Just keep looking at it," Dr. Atwal instructed me as the blinking light came back centered over my eye. A whirring sound was followed by the scanning white light again and then a beeping.

"You're going great Joella. Just 8 more seconds," the lady's voice said. A long beep happened and then the cylinder lifted from my eye.

I saw a glimpse of Dr. Atwal's face over me (<3) before he squirted two drops into my eye and put a Q-tip on my eye's surface. Then my eyesight blurred as it seemed he scrambled the surface of my eye like an egg. (Complete with "scrambling" noise) "OK. You did great. That eye is all done," he stated pleased as he put some sort of cover over it.

"Did I do OK? I was staring at the light, right? I saw it. Did it go ok?" I asked like a 5-year-old.

"You did awesome," he answered with a smile. "I'm a yeller so I would have let you know."

The same procedure happened to my left eye. I'm not sure if I goofed something up but I recall them deliberating softly to themselves before doing my right eye again. This time it was quicker. I'm sure they were just touching something up. It obviously wasn't serious (though at the time I was quietly concerned) because they never said anything and this morning, I had my follow-up and can see 20/20 using both eyes.

"OK. We're all done. You can sit up now," Dr. Atwal instructed me.

I slowly sat up and looked groggily at the team. "It's all blurry," I moaned softly, "Did I do OK? I was looking at the light the whole time."

Dr. Atwal smiled his boyish smile. "You did excellently. You are supposed to be a little blurry. How do you feel?"

Han Solo from "Star Wars" was literally the first thing that came into my head. "I feel terrible," I replied pained.

I felt a hand hold mine.

"You're all set. Come with me Joella," the lady's voice instructed me as I followed her out. She gave me my goodie bag with the same instructions as before, dark sunglasses, and reminded me that I was to come back for follow-up the next day. I looked at my phone and I was only in there for 15 minutes. It was now 3:15 PM.

My boyfriend took me to TGI Fridays pick up the lunch I ordered beforehand to celebrate this occasion, but I stayed in the car because my eyes were burning. I stayed awake until 5:30pm while using my drops before I asked him if he could get me ready for bed. He held my hand as we walked upstairs and gently taped my plastic eye guards over my eyes. I cooed softly as he tucked me in. I rustled the DC Amor diaper I had worn under my pajama pants for the procedure for comfort and protection since I had to drink 8 glasses of water before the procedure. I popped one of my pacifiers in my mouth and drifted off to sleep.

I woke up at 8:30pm with slightly blurred vision but could see significantly better. It was as if I had my glasses on and they were just dirty! I went outside and surveyed up and down my street. It was insane at how great I could see. All from a 15-minute PROCEDURE! (don't call it surgery).

CHAPTER 14
It's The Final Consult!

I TOOK MY nicotine & cotinine test July 21st. My script did not get sent over from Dr. Burke's office to Quest Diagnostics, so I was sitting in the exam room while the two phlebotomists were trying to find it. I'm panicking. I'm swearing. "Why can't these people do their fucking jobs! I asked her too and she said that I was all set!"

One of the ladies was like, "Don't worry, you have time before we close." She handed me a sticky note with a phone number on it. "Give them a call and have them fax it here."

I called Doctor Burke's office nearly in tears and the care coordinator said that she would send it over and assured me that Quest would receive it soon. I walked back into Quest feeling embarrassed about my blow up. I apologized and said, "Well that was very ladylike. You might as well change the F on my labels to M's."

The phlebotomist cracked up, "Oh my goodness, you're being

too hard on yourself." She then said she had gotten the fax and took my blood.

I waited for the results for a little over a week. I even made an account for them so that I could see my results ASAP. I logged in every day at least twice a day. It had been 44 days in total since I quit smoking. Would I finally pass?

On one of my results checks while I was at work, I finally saw the listing for July 21st.

Nicotine <2 - Cotinine <2

"Yes!" I shouted in the shop and ran to everyone like I had just hit a game winning homerun. "I passed! I passed!" They were happy and said things like "Great" and/or "You must be happy". I called the care coordinator and she had also gotten the results. She scheduled my final consultation for August 21st. Hopefully I was to make my date for my genital reassignment surgery then.

I anxiously waited for August 21st. I used my "Final Countdown" app on my phone and every day, no, every hour, I was closer to hopefully getting a date. The end of my physical dysphoria was in sight. Sure, I still had to work on my voice and mannerisms. I talked to Josie who I had worked with before on my voice two weeks prior. We talked on private video chat and she listened to me discuss where I was at in transitioning. She was also listening to my voice. I had my voice app open on my phone and I did hit the female and androgynous ranges a bit. However, most of the conversation had me in the male range. She explained how she was going to work with me, and we set up a date to get back to work.

August 21st finally came. I was extremely anxious. I knew Dr. Burke had to examine me, but I didn't know to what degree.

"What if he says it's too small and that it won't work?" I also was upset at myself for taking up smoking again because it set me back on making a date. "What if my date is like 5 more months away?"

James had taken the morning off so that he could take me since he had some questions. "Will you just relax. I'm sure everything is going to be fine."

I got all dolled up to go to the appointment. "I don't even know why I'm getting all made up," I said to him and sort of to myself also. "I'm superstitious. I know how these people work. I'm afraid they'll look at me if I show up in sweats and schedule me 9000 years out." I know this was not a fair character judgement. They were not "gatekeepers" the way the Center for Psychosexual Health felt.

We waited. And waited. James paced & looked at the big swivel examining light, the oxygen line, the intubater, and he rose and lowered the bed I was sitting on. I also paced around the room. I kept staring at myself on the wall mirror and admiring myself in the blue gown I was wearing. I was picturing myself laying in bed recovering from surgery and trying to see the woman that I was and soon would fully be. She blinked her blue eyes back at me and mimicked my movements.

"Purdy girl," James said to me as he watched.

"I look like a woman James," I said quietly as Joella stared back at me.

"Duh," James said which sort of ruined the surreal moment. I flopped back down on the bed and closed my eyes. I couldn't believe how close I was.

We were in the examining room for an hour and a half.

Dr. Burke knocked and entered the room. I hadn't seen him since November 2018, so I forgot what he looked like in those 9 months. "How are you doing?" he asked me as he stuck his hand out. I felt confused for a brief second (do women shake hands? umm yeah) and I shook his hand. James stood up to shake the doctor's hand as well. "So how has the not smoking been going?" Dr. Burke asked as he looked at me.

"Fine," I answered.

Doctor Burke nearly cut me off, "I bet you're like oh my God I need a cigarette," he said smiling.

"No," I said a little snippy, "the first week was hard and I felt unfocused but now I'm back to my old self."

Doctor Burke nodded, "Do you feel any different now that you don't smoke?"

I shook my head, "Not really, I bought zero nicotine juice for my vape," Dr. Burke looked a little skeptical, "But I barely use that anymore. The hand to mouth habit is practically gone."

Dr. Burke relaxed himself. "Well this appointment will take like 10 minutes and hopefully we will have a date for you. Do you mind if I take a look?" I clammed up for a minute.

"How do you want to do this?" I asked quietly.

"Well, standing up or sitting down. It doesn't matter," he replied nicely, "how about you just stand up for me."

I slowly stood up. "Ok now just lift up your gown for me." I lifted my gown up, closed my eyes, and looked away. I felt hands on my genitals. "Ok. I'm just checking for any hernias," Dr. Burke said, "give me a cough." I feebly coughed.

"I don't know what I'm doing," I softly muttered. I felt his hands move to the right side of my groin.

"And another cough," he said. I feebly coughed again.

"Ok. Everything is good. Any questions?" James and I asked a few questions about time to recover, driving, and dilation. Dr. Burke reiterated that my vagina would not be fully healed for about 3 months after surgery and I just had to be patient. "You'll be swollen, you'll be sore, you'll be red, you'll feel pretty beat up," he said. "It's not going to look maybe how you imagined it to look. We'll have you come back for a revision once you're healed. Nearly everyone gets a revision. We make a clitoral hood, do a labiaplasty..."

James nicely interjected, "Now is that something she will need to be stay overnight for or?"

Dr. Burke looked at me then at James, "No we do that outpatient. She will be fine."

It was very weird to hear myself called "she". I have no idea why. I mean I was a she. It's something I need to stop being so shocked about, I guess. Dr. Burke asked us if we had any more questions about the procedure. We both said "no" & he left.

The physician's assistant who dropped us off in the examining room re-entered. She had a clipboard. "October 8th," she simply said. I looked at her & my mouth dropped.

"Really? Oh my God," I said softly as I started crying.

"Ok. We have some paperwork to go over," she said, "you can sit down honey."

I sat back on the bed with tears in my eyes. "It's so close. End of September, early October like you said. I can't believe this." I sniffled as tears rolled down my cheeks. We went over the consent form which stated that I understood the risks of the procedure. I initialed the statements.

"Ok. We will see you 2 weeks before surgery," the PA said, "You are to stop any hormones and we will do some bloodwork on you. You will also get instructions for your bowel prep." I nodded and started softly crying again. "October 8th," she said again smiling.

"Yes," I said, "October 8th. It's so close."

"You're all set. You will get the packet in the mail for your pre-surgery exam." She left the room.

"October 8th," I whispered and sniffled as small tears still rolled down my soft female face.

CHAPTER 15
But Who Was J.?

I WAS DOING a lot of reflection with less than a month to go until my GRS. There's a park a mile from my house that I'd walk to and spin the Pokéstops while I'd read. I finished Susan Stryker's Transgender History and I found it informative. It put a lot into perspective and was humbling. I started reading Gender Outlaw by Kate Bornstein next and this paragraph hit home to me:

> I know I'm not a man- about that much I'm very clear, and I've come to the conclusion that I'm probably not a woman either, at least not according to a lot of people's rules on this sort of thing. (Bornstein, 2016)

See, it wasn't the surgery that was terrifying to me, it was fear that I was putting the cart before the horse. I was at the point where seeing myself *without* makeup still made me ecstatic. Through the 3.5 years of hormone replacement therapy, my face had become soft with no visible pores, my eyes were vibrant, my face was rounder with natural rosy cheeks, and I had fuller hair that was finally to a length I wanted. However, mentally I hadn't accepted it. I felt like my logic was holding me back. This couldn't be me. I didn't *feel* any different. I didn't feel like a woman.

But what does life as a woman *feel* like?

Shania Twain knows what it feels like to be a woman.

Apparently, being a woman is *being* a woman and the best thing about being a woman is the prerogative to have a little fun. To me, being a woman is trying to get my ponytail to stay while worrying about flyaways, trying to avoid drawing my eyeliner too low, readjusting my breasts in my bra, living with mood swings, needing cuddles, etc. et all. My prerogative to seek veracity was prohibitive and nonsensical.

IF I stopped hormone replacement therapy, I would need to get a double mastectomy, I'd remain sterile, and I've experienced such a paradigm shift in my sexuality that I'd never live as a man. I was never a man but at least I knew what I was trying to be…

My counselor turned that thought on its head.

"But who was J.?" she said in a session 20 days from my GRS date. I closed my eyes to think and couldn't come up with an answer. "Made you think, didn't I?" she said smiling.

I formed my answer hesitantly, and sounding like I had been lied to my entire life, "He wasn't really anything. Everything I did was because someone told me that I should."

A "eureka" moment flashed across her face. It was as if she had just caused a clinical breakthrough.

"Then why does it matter to let him go?" She answered aggressively, raising her voice at the end. She was challenging me.

"It matters…" I started and trailed off. I was visibly frustrated and becoming upset. Then I started grinning and laughing because she had tied me up. "Wait, what? Ask me again."

"Well you just said that everything you did was because someone else influenced you. So, who cares if you let that all go?" She answered animatedly throwing her hands up.

"Because I don't want to feel like I wasted 30 years of my life," I said with my head down.

"How was learning who you really were a waste?"

I scoffed. "Oh, don't give me that hippie, philosophical shit." I laughed, "Who was it? Einstein who said that 'when you stop learning is when you stop living' or something?"

Brianna shook her head. "Can't say I follow him."

"Well he's not exactly on Twitter," I started laughing, "Let's follow ole Al on the Twitters."

I cried a little later into our counseling session about not knowing who I am and not having anything to feel proud of. Brianna assured me that she'd be there to support me, and that I was strong enough to feel proud of myself. I drove down the street to this little truck stop diner I liked to frequent after sessions where I was upset. It was a quiet place where the servers called you "Hun" and they had good ole fashioned breakfast. I wrote a response to Brianna's question:

> *J. was a boy who played with girls in school when he was younger.*

He wanted to play flute or clarinet, but his mother said no.

The other boys never let him fully join their games, so he'd play for a bit and then hang around with the girls to listen to the gossip or play chase.

He got called "gay", "queer", and a "faggot" starting in 5th grade.

His parents told him that he was "a piece of shit", a "retard", that he "ruined their lives", and that they "didn't even want him".

His father choked him to the point where he'd go to school with bruises on his neck.

He'd lie to his 4th grade teacher about the bruises on his body from being choked and punched in the head, stomach, and back. He was even choked out.

He'd get beaten with a belt until he couldn't sit and slapped so hard his ears rang for hours.

He was told when he graduated from high school, "Now don't think you are hot shit or something".

He was told to "figure it out because you're not living here forever" when he came back from college.

He was told "you better go take your Zoloft" in a mocking way from his mother when he'd be upset.

His parents didn't even think to ask why he had the Zoloft, or why he/she sleeps with stuffed animals, or why he/she occasionally wear diapers to bed, or why he/she liked eyeliner, or why he hated haircuts, or if his first girl-

friend and him were having sex, or if he had a girlfriend to begin with...

The IDEA of who and what we all thought I was needs to be laid to rest. I lived as him and I tried my best, but I was never happy. That life was created from circumstance. That life was created from all the insecurities I was made to feel, the abandonment, the loneliness, and the abuse. That life was all I had. That life was all I knew. Now, I am Joella and I need to get over the fear of flying... for I am finally living.

PART 3

The Vagina Dialogs
Dated: October 2019- November 2019

Thank you to everyone who has communicated with me through this life-changing time:

My friend Andrea, it was nice to feel status quo and to have someone to text and not feel worried of judgement or if I was monopolizing our friendship.

My friend Brittany for visiting me and being supportive even though our ideologies on being transgender have deviations.

My boyfriend James for being such a supportive and loving partner. I looked forward to seeing my man each evening.

I thank all the staff at Erie County Medical Center for providing me the care I needed in order to recover from the surgery with dignity.

I would like to give an extra thanks to Jennifer (X). I feel we spent the most time together and your plucky, yet caring heart really hit home to me. You made me feel as if I could do it (recovery). You made me feel like a young woman starting to live life anew.

CHAPTER 1
Surgery Day

The author would like to inform her readers that this section is from daily journals while she was at the hospital for gender affirmation vaginoplasty. They have been neither edited or addended.

I LAID IN my hospital bed trying to type up the experience of gender affirming vaginoplasty. I arrived in the pre-op wing at 8am where I donned my gown and yellow anti-slip socks. I was extremely calm and ready as I put what I was wearing into the shiny garment bag labeled "patient belongings".

The anesthesiologist entered my partition and was about to get my IV ready before 2 other nurses showed up. "Did you need any help?" this tall skinny brunette girl asked.

There was a blonde male with a surfer beard next to her who apparently wanted to help too. "Do you mind if I do it? I need numbers," he asked.

I became apprehensive. I still hate needles, despite having to do routine bloodwork for my hormone levels every six months and what the heck does 'I need numbers' mean?

"Is he any good?" I asked the tall skinny brunette.

She smirked, "He's alright," she answered.

The anesthesiologist nodded in agreement. The blond guy came over to me and proceeded to wrap the tourniquet around my right arm. He then started feeling my forearm for the vein and slid the needle in. "Well you were right to ask," he said humorously, "I missed it there."

He missed! I knew he would because I can never take an IV there! Although to his defense, my veins probably weren't in the best condition after going 8 plus hours without anything by mouth. I got upset and was nearly in tears, "We're off to great start," I moaned. The tall skinny girl gave the guy a dirty look.

"Let her do it," the anesthesiologist said sternly. The guy unwrapped the tourniquet from my arm making a loud rubber-band snap. "You're supposed to... [can't remember what she said] ... first," she said firmly to him. The tall skinny girl came over and wrapped the tourniquet on. She went for the good vein. The one inside the elbow. It works every time. The needle slid in smoothly and she replaced it with the thin plastic tube.

"OK needle's out, you're all set," she said as she stared down the blonde guy with a cute little 'I win' smirk.

I laid there and waited and waited. Dr Burke showed up and said, 'good morning.'

"Look at youuuuu," I said impressed as I looked him up and

down. He looked super cute with a sweater and dark jeans on.

He scribbled his initials on a bunch of pages in my binder. "I'll see you soon, ok?" he said nicely as he departed.

The anesthesiologist came back. "Ok Joella, I'm going to give you something to keep you feeling calm. It'll make you feel like you had a few glasses of wine or cocktails." I nodded and she shot the tube into my IV line. That was the last thing I remember before starting to come-to back in the same wing.

I remember drunkenly asking, "Did you even do it?" and a voice responded, "Yes everything went well." Then my legs started violently shaking uncontrollably as I was becoming semi-conscious. "I can't stop shaking!" I yelled as my blurry vision saw a bunch of heads over me.

"It's ok, it's ok," this man's voice reassured me, "it's just adrenaline, you're ok."

I continued shaking for a long while, I was gasping for breath, and I was in pain. "Oh my God, it hurts so bad!" I yelled.

"Give her some morphine!" another voice called out. I fell asleep for a second. I became conscious shortly after and was still violently shaking. All the heads over me were gone.

There was just this older blond schoolmarm looking woman left at the desks. "What are you doing? You need to cough and breathe!" she chastised me.

Like jeez, I'm sorry. I'm just waking up from being chemically paralyzed with a tube down my throat. Pardon me that I'm only semi-conscious and gasping for air.

I started to calm down and breathe the oxygen from my nostril thingy. I remember the older blonde nurse was annoyed because I apparently went through almost 3 tanks of oxygen.

"I'm going to get you something for your leg tremors and get your boyfriend," she said. I woke up from another snooze as James was sauntering into my curtained off area. We talked about how it went. I waited 5 hours in the recovery area from my room to be ready. Dr. Burke likes this one wing so that's where he puts his patients. I didn't mind. I was going to be there for a week and in bed for most of it anyway. What difference did the change in scenery make?

CHAPTER 2
The Young and The Rested

WEDNESDAY AND THURSDAY were a little more eventful, albeit I was still on bed rest in my room until Friday. My vagina was covered by 2 strips of shiny rubbery tape that looked like a microskirt across my hips with bandages covering my vagina underneath. I mostly slept on and off that day an hour at a time. I felt very groggy but peaceful throughout. I was on a regular diet, so I was able to eat off the menu. The first day I picked at my meals. I had a few forkfuls of scrambled eggs, a few forkfuls of home fries, and 2 sausage patties. The sausage was the highlight. Good ole greasy fat. Yummy! My first bite into one and I literally went like "ahhh" in ecstasy. I had this dry ass chicken salad that I barely touched for lunch. The chicken was like eating a glue filled sponge. Then excruciating giant gas bubbles erupted in my stomach late afternoon. Honestly, they were more painful than the surgery site! They were loud and the pressure was pushing onto my vagina. I declined anything for dinner due to lack of appetite.

I had my vitals checked every 2 hours throughout Wednesday by the staff, and thankfully, my pain level was at only a 3 or 4 for me because my blood pressure was too low for morphine. I managed my pain with Tylenol supplemented by a Norco here and there. The nurses were extremely impressed with my progress that I was wiggling around in bed with minimal pain. I felt strong. I was optimistic.

I was off the strict vital checks on Thursday, and as a result I was able to get more consistent sleep. I was starting to pass gas in the middle of the night which alleviated my stomach cramps. It was so gross. They were drawn out farts, but they didn't smell so thank goodness. My pain level was less than the day before. I would say that I was at a 3 and sometimes only a 2. My blood pressure was still too low for morphine, but I was doing great with just the Tylenol. By dinnertime we learned that I hadn't taken any Norco for 36 hours. I took one before bed just to help me sleep and keep my pain level at the low level I was at.

The following morning, I was feeling stronger and was able to fully sit up in bed and wiggle myself into position for breakfast. "I did it!" I exclaimed raising my arms in victory.

"Yeah you did," the nurse PJ said, "you're doing really well."

I also ate more than the prior morning. I had a bowl of cream of wheat, a yogurt, and a slice of bacon. My taste buds seemed to be still tasting things as bland, and my sense of smell was very different. The bacon made feel nauseous when I first smelled it.

The Vagina Dialogs

The smell was very powerful. I listened to sports talk radio on my phone as I picked at my brekky and it felt like I was doing my regular breakfast routine. After breakfast my energy level crashed, and I was exhausted. I got shifted around and dozed on and off.

Lunch got delivered while I was asleep and in my groggy state, I almost gave it to nurse PJ to take away thinking it was my breakfast. "No, no, this is your lunch, sweetheart," he said gently.

"Oh, oh my God, I'm just so groggy," I said.

"Yeah, they delivered it to you when you were asleep," he peeked under the lid, "looks good too! Stuffed shells. I'll let them know to leave it with you a bit."

"Ok. Thanks," I replied sleepily. I then hit the recline button to sit my bed up. I listened to another segment of sports talk radio and picked at lunch before feeling exhausted again. I let my bed down, wiggled around to get snuggly, and dozed off.

James had been visiting me after work each night and Thursday I was a lot more mentally available. He grabbed my hairbrush and brushed my hair without me even asking and put my earrings back in. He looked at me lovingly. "You look great hun", he said. I had him use one of my bath wipes to wash my back since I only managed to do my front. It was refreshing to wash the sweat off. "Oh my God, today was crazy" I talked very animated as he finished my back and I rolled back over.

"Yeah? What happened?" he asked.

"Well fricking there was this lady who kept puking for like 3 hours last night. It was so gross. Then this afternoon, there was a guy who got stabbed and his friend got shot."

James raised his eyebrows. "Yeah? Is he ok?"

"Yeah, it was frigging crazy. He was talking about it to someone on the phone that he was in the 'ambyoulance' and that he was dead for a bit like flatlined for 20 seconds and they gave him a shot and like 'woo' he came back to life and he had a hole in his neck and when he'd breathe he could hear the air whistle. But it was so crazy how cavalier he was talking about it! Like it was just some regular day at the office," I ended chuckling.

James looked shocked," That's crazy. Damn." Then we talked about his day at work while watching the WNBA final. I felt sleepy at like 9:30 and we kissed bye as I feel asleep.

CHAPTER 3
The 2-Step Woozie

I SLEPT WELL enough due to the medication and woke up right before the doctor came in. "You ready to do this? Today's the big day," he said happily.

I groaned as I was still waking up. "It's not going to hurt is it?"

He smiled warmly, "It may be a little uncomfortable since we're moving down there but nothing horrible. We're going to take out the Foley. That's probably going to be the most uncomfortable. You may feel a little burn." He was right. The nurse disconnected my Foley and removed it.

I felt a quick burn and some wetness drip. "Oh no, did I pee?" I asked embarrassedly.

"It's ok, it happens. You have a pad under you," the doctor said. I then felt the tape being removed from my hip and it felt super sensitive at my vaginal area. I moaned. "You ok?" he asked looking concerned at me.

"It just feels weird," I moaned, "it's super sensitive."

The doctor nodded as he gestured for me to roll on my side. He manipulated the tape off from over my butt, "Well that's actually really good then. Ok take a breath and relax", he said as he slowly returned me onto my back and pulled the bandage down between my vagina. I felt a slight burning and moisture. I looked down at her for the first time. The bandage covering it was laid face up and was coated in goop and dried blood. My vagina had a few stitches on each side. What shocked me were the two hoses connected to my drains on the wall. Just sticking out of the top of my mound. I felt like a mutant or some alien creature. Despite that shock, I was happy. She was beautiful and she was my vagina.

My recovery picked up the pace when I finally got out of bed. Well, after my first try anyway. I had finished breakfast at 9am and the nurses came in to help me out of bed. "Ok we're going to try to get to the bathroom and have you pee." I was nervous about moving into the great wide open since I hadn't viewed what the full extent of my room was like. They took my leg balloons off, lowered my rails, and gently took hold my ankles. "Ok can you swing yourself around? I had been moving around in the bed well. This was going to be easy! I swung my legs around and sat at the edge. I moaned as a wave of exhaustion washed over me. My butt felt weird and I obviously had packing in my vagina. It was overall a very weird feeling of groin pressure and knowing that I was without my penis. "Take some deep breaths," one of the nurses said. I inhaled and they each grabbed my hands and I stood up for the first time in 49 hours.

Dizziness washed over me, and I felt like I had drunk a bottle of booze. "Omg I feel terrible!" I sniffled and started to cry.

"Are you ok? Does it hurt?" A nurse asked.

"No, it just feels weird. I feel terrible," I yowled.

"Well just relax and we'll take a few steps."

I took two steps before I began teetering, my ears starting ringing, and my vision got bright dots in front of it. "I'm going down, I'm going down!" I cried out.

They were quick to each get an arm around my back. "You're OK, you're OK. Just lay back down. You did great." They helped me swing my legs back on the bed as my vision was blurry. I honestly thought I was dying. My first thought as I was nearly fainting was how dumb it was to get this surgery if my body was just going to go into shock and die. My vision cleared up quickly and I felt fully conscious again. "Yeah, I saw all of the color drain out of you. But you did great. We'll keep trying. Let us know when you're ready. We have to get you out of bed and peeing," the nurse said. I nodded and started crying. I felt like a failure. Nurse Jennifer came over to the bedside. "Now, now don't cry. You did awesome. You just had a major surgery. You'll get there." She grabbed my hand as I sniffed back tears. I smiled and she smiled back. "There's that smile. Call me when you're ready." She departed and I slowly drifted off to sleep.

CHAPTER 4
The Stupid Chair

It was a little after noontime when lunch came. I ordered a cheeseburger and annihilated it. My appetite was accelerating back to normal. The nurse Jennifer came in shortly after. "You ready to try again?" she asked, "we don't want to put the Foley back in." That was the motivation I needed to hear. I also was feeling back to normal after my burger and Pepsi. I think the caffeine helped get me focused and helped eliminate the nagging headache I had for a day and a half. Jennifer lowered my rail, disconnected my IV, and clipped my drains to my gown. I began swinging my legs over the edge of the bed. She gently guided me as I sat up with my feet on the floor.

I started feeling dizzy. "Ok, just give me a second please," I said as I put some pressure through my calves to the floor and looked around the room.

"Sure, take your time, get oriented," she answered nicely. I wiggled and slowly stood up. "Nice and slow now," Jennifer said with her hand ready to catch me. I began waddling as I brushed my hand along the wall. I felt like I was moving 100 mph. I was elated.

"Ok, just sit there," Jennifer said as I faced a little bathroom. There was a toilet with handrails on each side with a pull rope in the left wall that said, "pull for assistance". Off to my right (from sitting on the toilet) was a shower head with a drain and one of those cloth baskets hampers on casters. I relaxed and waited. I felt pressure like I was holding back urine on a long car ride. Then I heard tinkling in the toilet as the pressure slowly alleviated.

"I'm peeing! I'm peeing!" I said excitedly sounding like a kid potty training.

"Good! Yeah, I hear you," Jennifer said from the sink outside the door.

I finished peeing and she handed me a squeezy bottle with sterile water. "Ok you're going to gently squirt yourself down and blot," she demonstrated as she squirted the water on me for a second. The warm water felt soothing on my vagina. She went back to clean up my bedding as I rinsed.

Jennifer came back to bathroom as dizziness overcame me. "Ugh, I need to lay down. I'm exhausted," I groaned. I then became disappointed in myself because I know she wanted me to wash myself up and sit in the reclining chair next to my room's big windows. I had to remind myself that I *did* manage to walk and go pee.

"Ok, we'll try again later to get you cleaned up and sitting down. We can't have you lying in bed all day." I nodded.

"I know, I'm sorry but I *went* pee. I'll get to the chair in a little bit. How about 2pm?" I said as I looked at the clock. I wanted to set this goal for myself.

"Alright, you're doing well. I'm going to hold you to it," Jennifer chuckled.

"I know how you feel about the stupid chair," I said smiling. She departed and I dozed off for an hour.

I called for Jennifer using the 'nurse' button on my bed's siderail a little after 2pm. She got me up and I moved a lot swifter to the edge of the bed. There was pressure around my vagina as I moved but I figured it was merely that I was still stuffed with the packing. I grabbed the handrail at the headboard and pulled myself to my feet. I felt good. I was steady. I did "the waddle" to the bathroom and sat. I wiggled a little and widened my legs. Ooh, that felt better. I felt centered and there was very little pressure on my groin. I began peeing and the stream went straight down into the toilet. I felt super proud.

Jennifer came to help after I squirted myself down and gently blotted. She brought me to the sink, and I brushed my teeth. She had a little thing of roll-on deodorant and I used some soapy sponge bath wipes to wipe myself off before applying it to my underarms. I gazed over my reflection in the mirror and loved the woman I was. "I actually look cute," I said elated.

"Yeah, you look good. Let's fix your hair," Jennifer said.

"Well I can make it to the stupid chair now," I snarked.

Jennifer laughed, "OK let's have you sit on the bed and I'll get it ready." She prepped the recliner with a pad, sheet, and pillow for my butt. I grabbed my hairbrush and my can of dry shampoo. I then eased myself into the chair and she stuck the leg rest out. It jarred me a bit with the pressure change, but I relaxed with it. I was sitting! I sprayed my hair and brushed it out. It felt a lot better.

For the rest of the evening, Jennifer came when I called for a nurse to help me make it to the bathroom. It was always such a process to set me into bed or get me out of bed. First, I had a tube coming from the upper left and a tube coming from the upper right of my vaginal mound that connected to a drain bulb which was connected to wall suction. The nurse would have to disconnect the drain bulbs from wall suction and then clamp them to my gown. Many a time they would be clamped lower than I would like which resulted in a sensation comparable to if a toddler grabbed a man's testicle and pulled downward. Secondly, they would have to remove these Velcro-on air balloons that wrapped around each calf and were attached to a compressor at the foot of the bed. Finally, they'd lower my left siderail and watch as I wiggled and lifted myself out of bed.

Jennifer came to change my gown at 6:30pm and, for the first time, I was nude and prepared to see myself. I was sitting on my butt on the edge of the bed and looked down at myself. I admired my boobs, my tummy, and my healing vagina. I was a woman. My body was beautiful and the way I wanted it to be.

CHAPTER 5
Can They Print the Word "Clitoris"?

IT WAS SATURDAY when I was awoken at 6am by the urologist who was on my surgery team. "Hello, my name is Eugene [can't remember] (I swear it was like Dostoyevsky, or some shit) I was the urologist during your surgery. Do you mind if I take a look at you?" he asked.

It was nice of him to ask. In fact, everyone was so responsive, respectful, and just nice. I was apprehensive at first since I was so sensitive down there. In fact, I was so sensitive that my vagina was the first body part that noticed any sort of room temperature change. I like a cold room, optimally 67-68 degrees for sleep, so I'd fall asleep with just my gown covering me and let her air out. Once my vagina got cold, the rest of me got cold in no time. "You gotta do what you gotta do," I smiled and stretched. I was still laying down since I had just woken up.

The Vagina Dialogs

The urologist stood over me and moved his head at various angles. He took his first two fingers and lightly pressed in spots on my groin. I just laid watching and he went to my left labia. Something felt weird. I breathed in quickly. "You ok?" he asked.

"Yeah just felt weird," I responded, "not pain just like nerves."

He nodded, "This labium is more swollen than the other, but it all looks good."

He then gently slid the labium over, and I squealed out. "Oh my God," I called out.

The urologist looked flustered, "Wh-what did I do? I was already touching there before."

I gasped the sensation away, "I don't know. It just felt weird like when someone tickles you too much. I don't know how to explain it. It didn't hurt, don't worry," I reassured him.

He shook his head clearly confused. He continued visually inspecting me as he talked, "But I was touching there before. Maybe I wasn't so ginger on that last movement..." his voice trailed off.

"What?" I asked with some concern.

He had a look of pleasant surprise on his face. "You know what's over there?" He asked quizzically. I shook my head and looked like *no, I don't, Dr. Fingers this is my first vagina installa*tion.

He began slowly, "It's... your clitoris. It's just slightly angled because of the swelling and you're not used to things being in a little different formation."

A Cheshire cat grin flashed across my face. "My clitoris? Oh shit. No wonder," I said shocked.

He smiled, "Well, everything looks great. Just some swelling that will continue to get better. I want you to try and hike around. Take it easy, don't run a marathon or anything but you need to walk around the wing to get good blood flow."

I nodded sagely, "Ok will do!" I answered cheery. He gave me like a "peace sign" wave and departed. I stared at the ceiling with a wide ass grin still on my face.

James came and visited Saturday afternoon. We watched this show called "Ridiculousness". I was laughing so hard/trying not to laugh so my area wouldn't stretch that a nurse came to ask if I was ok.

Following orders, James and I went for four walks down the hall, around a corner, to a large viewing window during his visit. I was on the seventh floor, so I had a great view. We watched the show, had dinner, and he left when I started to get tired. I slept the best I had since arriving at the hospital. I was still only sleeping an hour at a time due to constantly having to pee, but I was tallying more hours.

CHAPTER 6
Pains, Drains, & Bantermobiles

SUNDAY MORNING WAS full of milestones beginning with my nerves decided they wanted to wake up down there. I woke up to go pee and it felt like someone was playing "Flight of the Bumblebee" off my vagina. It was electrical. Peeing felt intense and caused me to moan. Thankfully, I wasn't in pain. The urologist Dr. E knocked and entered around 8am. My eyes fluttered and I slowly awoke. "Morning," he said, "May I take another look?"

I looked at his University at Buffalo fleece. It had his name on it. "So, where's your last name from?" I asked brightly.

He glanced at me as I was removing my covers. "I'll give you 2 guesses and then I get to yell at you," he said playfully.

I didn't realize how quiet and intelligent his voice sounded until today. Doc should do ASMR on the side. I pondered, "Well it should be Russian, but you don't seem Russian."

He smirked and started looking around at my vagina. "What do you mean?" He asked amused.

"Oh, I don't know I always pictured Russian men to be more gruff or stiff," I answered.

"Well you have to consider where I work," he said as he intently examined me, "I have to be quiet and nicer at a hospital."

I moved my eyes reflexively, "Yeah, that's true."

"When I go home, I yell. At my wife. In my Russian voice," he quickly responded. I cracked up laughing. "Ok. So, what I want to do is take a drain out today," he said in thought looking at the two tubes branching off the top of my vagina.

I felt like we were about to defuse a bomb. "Which one?" I asked happily.

"The right one," he answered, "I'm hoping it will be easy. It looks like..." he paused and gently touched, "...it is right on top and I can slide it right out. It'll feel like someone pulling a long straw out of your abdomen." I stared up at him quizzically. "Not that anyone experiences that frequently," Dr. E quickly finished glancing at my expression. I laughed again.

I took long breaths as he began pulling the tube out of me. I noticed his Ohio State lanyard. "Ohio state eh?" I asked and smirked, "now do you call it Ohio State or THE Ohio State?"

Dr. E stopped pulling a second and looked over, "I call it THE Ohio State, as should you," he answered sternly. I laughed and he resumed pulling the drain out. It didn't take long, and he held the hose off to my side. "That much was in you," he said with a hand on the lower end. It was over a foot of tubing.

My eyes were wide, "Holy shit, that's going to feel better."

He nodded and connected the left drain back to suction. "Everything looks great, you're just swollen, but it's going to look better and better. Get moving today. I'm going to run your labs from today. Your blood count is low and if your blood pressure is still low the way it's been, you may have to get a transfusion." I looked upset. "Well don't worry about it, I still have to check," he said, "have a good day."

"You too," I said back, and he turned and departed my room.

CHAPTER 7
Lightning Crashes

THINGS FLOWED SMOOTHLY the rest of the day on Sunday. The Buffalo Bills were on a bye week so there wasn't any football on, at least that I cared to watch. I asked the nursing staff that morning if there was a way I could go outside and walk more. They were very excited that I asked and informed me to call them when I was ready, so they could bring me a wheelchair to sit in outside since I wasn't allowed to sit on hard and germy park benches. James came to visit that afternoon and I let him know the good news.

We went to the nursing station and one of the nurses left and returned with a wheelchair that looked like it was straight out of the late '70s. I hopped in and James wheeled me off the unit, into the elevator, and around about eleven different hallways to the outside of the hospital. I hopped out and James handed me my cane. It was a beautiful fall day, mid 60's, sunny, with that crisp smell in the air, and a gentle breeze. It was nice to be out of the hospital considering I hadn't been outside since getting in and out of the car for surgery five days prior. I began slowly walking with James pushing the wheelchair next to me to a building one of the nurses said had flowers. There was an older man in a wheelchair off to our right sitting in the sun near the curb and he looked over at me with a big grin on his face.

"Oooooh, some-body had a bay-bay," he said excitedly. I looked over and beamed a huge smile. He looked at the two of us smiling and James and I continued our walk.

I was giddy, "Did you hear him?" I snickered to James. "I still look female with this gown, my hair's a mess, and I have no make-up on?"

James just shook his head, "Honey, you're a female. You just had a baby. How do you want to look?" He finished with his boyish smirk.

I laughed. "Well if anyone asks, it was a girl," I pointed and wagged my finger up and down.

"Of course," James said goofily.

I managed to walk to the next building before getting tired. James had me hop into the wheelchair and we rested outside in the sun. After our break, he rolled me to the third building which was the long-term care facility that allegedly had flowers. Well, it did have flowers. It also had paving stones. With peoples' names on them and when they died. I hopped out of the wheelchair and walked around.

"Jeez, this is depressing," James said.

"I know right!" I exclaimed as I read the inscriptions on the memorial stones and flower placards. I began getting tired and hopped back into the wheelchair. "Ok. Let's get back inside, I'm getting tired," I said gently.

James nodded, "Ok hon." He wheeled me back to the hospital entrance, through the eleven different hallways, back to the elevator, and back onto our wing. A nurse was near my room with a med-cart. She turned and saw us.

"Oh! How'd you do?" She asked excitedly.

"Well I walked from the entrance here to the second building. What is that? The ambulatory one? Then James wheeled me to the long-term care building, and we walked around. Finally, I got tired and he wheeled me back up here."

The nurse nodded and seemed impressed. "That's great and oh yeah, the physical therapist was looking for you. He said he'll be back in a second." I tilted my head inquisitively. The nurse noticed my confusion. "He just wants to see how you are moving to see when you can be discharged. Judging by how you did, you're fine."

I smiled, "Good, I'm getting ready to gooooooo," I finished with emphasis. I returned to my room and the PT guy came in shortly after.

"Knock, knock. Hi Joella, I'm the physical therapist here on this unit. Do you mind if we go for a quick walk and do an exercise? I just want to see how you're moving around."

I nodded and smiled, "We should do well. My boyfriend and I just came back from a walk outside."

I began walking next to the physical therapist. He looked impressed and dropped the arm he was holding in case I was unsteady. "Oh! Well that's great. Let's just go to the end of the hall." I walked with my cane to the end of the hall. "Ok. Now wait a minute," he said as he looked perplexed at me and the cane.

"What's wrong?" I asked. I was hoping he wasn't going to yell at me for cheating or something.

"Nothing really. You're moving well. I don't think you need that," he finished as he nodded towards my cane.

I looked down at the cane. "You're probably right. It just helps me last longer. It's literally twice as tiring to walk without it."

He nodded receptively. "Well for the sake of this exercise, how about we walk back down the hall without it. I have another quick thing we need to do too. Does your home have any stairs?"

I nodded as I walked back down the hall with the physical therapist, "Yeah, I have two to get to the door and a bunch to get to the second floor."

"OK. Let's stop here. I have a stair under this cubby so we can see how you're doing with that." He slid a long stepstool with grippy tape on the top of it out in front of me. I got a little nervous. "What you're going to do is just take a few steps up and down, leading with your right foot," he instructed me. I stepped up and down on the stair as he instructed. "Good. Now try it again, this time lead up with your left foot." I raised my left leg and grimaced as I stepped onto the stair.

"Ugh. That doesn't feel too good," I winced as I stepped back off the stair, "It's sore when I go that way."

The physical therapist nodded, "Sometimes that happens when

you have a bad leg and a good leg. Are you more swollen or something on that left side?"

"Yeah, they pointed that out a few days ago," I replied.

The physical therapist hummed in agreement. "Well let's just try that left foot a couple more times." I went up and down the step with a few pained expressions. "Ok. Stop. There's a little trick when you go home to not be so sore." I looked up at him intently. "It's 'upwards to heaven, downwards to hell', so what you want to do is lead with your good leg (he slapped his right leg) as you go up the stairs, and lead with the bad leg as you go down."

I was amazed. "Oh wow! That's super cool. You're the expert."

He smiled wide, "Try that and see. Step onto the stair with your right and step off starting with your left."

I followed his instruction. I didn't feel pain as I stepped off the stair. "That's great! I don't feel sore anymore."

The physical therapist looked proud of himself. "Fantastic. Remember that when you are home." He slid the stair back into the cubby near the nursing station. "I don't see any reason why we'd be worried about you going home. I'll write up my notes. Good luck with everything," he finished as he nodded to me.

"Well thanks so much for the tidbit. I'll definitely remember that!" I walked back to my room where James was sitting in the recliner. "Everything went well, and I learned a trick for stairs," I said excitedly.

"Oh yeah?" James said raising an eyebrow, "and what's that?"

"Well he said to go up the stairs starting with my right leg and go down the stairs starting with my left. It really worked so that I'm not sore."

"Good, good," James said relaxed, "things are coming along."

We watched TV and walked to the window a few times before he left to go home, and I went to bed.

CHAPTER 8
Homeward Bound

My antibiotic IV was finished that night and I had even asked if I could stop wearing my air pillows on my calves. The nurse was hesitant, but I pleaded with her that I was taking walks, so we didn't have to worry about blood clots, right? She agreed and turned the compressor off and disconnected the air pillows. Therefore, I only had my left drain connected to me.

Dr E. returned the following morning to check up on me. This time there wasn't any fun banter. He informed me we were taking out the left drain. I remember feeling liberated and he mentioned something like I wouldn't need to be tethered to the wall anymore. The drain was removed, and he taped a foam square over the hole. He said that he checked my labs and that I wouldn't need a transfusion. He said my blood count came back quickly, and I was in the clear. I was relieved. He gave me a quick 'good luck' and left. I was slightly disappointed that we didn't have any witty conversation, but I was happy to be free of lines and cables.

I sauntered to the nurses' station later that morning and asked if I could be discharged. The one nurse seemed taken aback by this request, but I pleaded my case.

"I mean, there's nothing left for me to do here," I stated, "I'm walking around, I have nothing connected to me anymore, I'm going to the bathroom fine, and my blood count is back to normal. I'm ready to go home."

The nurse chuckled, "You just want to get out of here and leave us huh? I'll talk to the discharge planner and let her know you want to go home."

"Thanks," I said in my sweetest 'Ella voice' as I turned heel back to my room.

The nurse came in later that morning with my meds. "Sooooo, I have good news!" she said. I nearly jumped off the bed. "I heard back from the discharge planner and she's going to let you go home today."

I raised my arms in victory, "Yes! I'm so ready. It'll be nice to get some sleep. It's just crazy. I'm only sleeping for two hours at a time because ten people come in before 9am."

The nurse chuckled as she handed me my medicine cup. "Yeah I can see how that would be annoying but we're just checking on you."

"Oh I know," I said gulping down the medications, "But it's like the maintenance guy comes in to empty the garbage, the sharps lady comes in, the urologist comes in, you come in, nutrition comes in, the tooth fairy-Easter bunny-Santa Claus, and the doctor all come in! The nurse laughed as I finished waving my hands. "And that's all before 8 o'clock in the morning!"

"Well you'll be sleeping home tonight. We'll make sure you're all set later this afternoon," she said as she wheeled her cart out and to the next room.

Apparently, my appetite was back in full force because when breakfast came, I ate it ravenously. James arrived in the afternoon and we went outside for a walk since we had the wheelchair parked in my room from the day before. I filled him in on the good news. I went a lot farther without needed to rest and we returned inside, and I plopped back onto the bed.

The discharge planner visited with a big packet of information. "So, you're leaving us today?" she said with her hands on her hips in a mock pout.

"Yeah, I'm ready to go," I said lazily as I stretched in bed.

The planner riffled through the packet. "So, this has everything you need to know specific to *your* surgery," she said with emphasis. I nodded. "There's instructions on care, who to call if you have an emergency, and just what we did here at the hospital. So that's for you and take your time. We're not kicking you out or anything," she finished with a laugh.

"Oh, um, one thing," I began quietly. She turned back around.

"Yes, what's up?" she asked nicely.

I grabbed the pillow from behind my head and scrunched it in my arms. "Can I have this pillow?" It's the most comfortable pillow I've ever had. ---and I don't have any underwear or pads with me,"

I looked at her meekly with a 'Cindy Lou Who' on my face. She looked at me as I hugged the pillow. "I didn't see anything," she whispered, "and follow me, I'll go grab you something to wear." I hopped out of the bed and followed her to a little supply closet. She grabbed a plastic wrapped package that was labeled 'maternity underwear' and she grabbed a maxi pad from a package. She seemed satisfied and handed me them. "There you go. Like I said. No rush. I'm glad everything went so well."

I smiled, "Thank you so much. Everyone was amazing and so helpful." I walked across the way to the nurses' station said my goodbyes and thanked everyone for taking good care of me. I walked back to my room where James was picking up and packing my suitcase. I removed my gown and slowly began getting dressed. I brought this t-shirt I got in sixth grade at 'graduation' which was still three sizes too long and some baggy workout pants. I stopped to admire myself in the mirror. Everything felt so right with my body.

We left the hospital soon after. I rode in the car while sitting on this inflatable 'donut' cushion for hemorrhoids and stuff. The ride wasn't too bad. There were a few bumps and I even encouraged James to drive normally.

"You don't have to drive like a grandma," I pointed out as he got onto the highway. He turned quickly at me with a look on his face and shrugged.

"Well jeez. I didn't want to hurt you or anything," he answered exasperated. He sped up the car onto the ramp.

"Weeeeee," I exclaimed, "See you are fine. It's a Toyota. It's comfortable as heck."

We pulled into Burger King for lunch since I was craving a Whopper in a bad way before heading home.

I had a little adjustment period getting used to our house. The first issue was in the bathroom. The toilet at the hospital had a riser on it so that you didn't have to bend over to sit. No such luck with ours.

"Oh shit! This sucks!" I yelled from the bathroom.

"What? What's wrong?" James asked from downstairs.

I was pissed and upset, "The frigging toilet is too low. Oh my God, this hurts." I splayed my legs out and tried to hunker down. I managed to pee and had to grab the sink next to me in order to haul myself back up.

The second issue was the stairs. Sure, the 'upwards to heaven, downwards to hell' trick helped but it was still exhausting to go up and down. I was taking one step at a time in the first days of being home. That also got to me emotionally.

Finally, there was my bed. Thankfully, James grabbed me a sturdy two-step stool that I dubbed my 'princess steps' in order to get into my bed. The real issue was that I didn't have the convenient electronic controls to raise and lower the head and body of the bed as well as the various handholds on railings and headboards.

I began to cry that night as I was exhausted. "This sucks," I wailed, "I didn't think about any of this before I asked to come home."

James stood over me as he tucked me in. "You are ok honey; you are getting better already. Think about it. You're already over the hump."

I sniffled back my tears and weakly smiled. "Yeah, you're right. I just didn't realize how hard it was going to be. I'll be ok. At least I'll get some real sleep."

James nodded and kissed my forehead. "Yep, get some sleep. Let me know if you need help." He left to go to his room, and I fell asleep soon after.

CHAPTER 9
Over the Hump

THE FIRST WEEK of being home was spent resting and adjusting to the new surroundings. My pattern was sit/walk for two hours and then feel exhausted and need to nap for two hours. My urine stream was everywhere as Dr. Burke and my friends warned me beforehand, so I stood/squatted in the bathtub to pee. However, that was convenient since I could just fill up the peri-bottle and rinse myself off. To get in and out of bed I would grab the bedpost, twist myself onto my side, and haul myself onto my hands and knees. Then I backed myself out of bed like a tractor trailer onto my 'princess stairs'. Sleeping was atrocious. I couldn't lay on my side since my vulva hurt so I was reduced to sleeping on my back which I frigging hate. I had a pillow under my feet, a u-shaped body pillow under my right leg and my stuffed alpaca named Paxton under my left leg. At least I was in my own bed.

The Vagina Dialogs

Everything was healing well the start my second week at home. My labia began spreading open like wings and seemed to know where to rest on my body. I had some vaginal discharge and I was constantly bemoaning that it smelled 'medically'. I wore pads to stay sanitary. At this point, I was almost mad? at myself for getting the surgery. I described it to people as being 'in shock'. I was very conflicted. I felt like I was missing an appendage but at the same point I was happy it was gone.

Moving around in bed was easier but I was still forced to sleep on my back.

Then one day when I was getting up to go to the bathroom my packing fell out.

I was panicked for two reasons. One, my vaginal opening scared me because it was wet with blood and seemed gaping to me. Secondly, the packing which was made of gauze and shaped like a butt-plug was attached to my body by stitches. It was saturated in ooze and blood and it smelled 'medically'. I dialed Dr. Burke's office who told me to try and slide it back into me. So, I waddled back to my room with my hands cupping this wet and squishy phallus-shaped wad of gauze that was attached to my vulva and laid down. I had no idea how to go about this. I tried to finagle it into the cavity, but the mummy dildo began to unravel. I felt helpless and started to cry.

My saving grace was that James was on his way home from work. I decided that I would just cut the mummy phallus off my body and pray that my vaginal canal didn't vacuum seal itself before next week's follow-up appointment. I texted James and told him that I needed his help. He arrived while I was drying my tears and sniffling. We experienced a scene like in *Iron Man* where Tony Stark is instructing Pepper Potts how to remove the old reactor in his chest and replace it with the new one. Only James was Pepper. The mummy dick was removed from my body leaving strands of stitching and I called Dr. Burke's office to let them know the news. They instructed me to start douching my neo-vagina out and to not worry.

James and I went to Rite-Aid and bought an old-school douchebag with the hose and various attachments. I didn't realize that a douchebag was like a Shark vacuum.

I read on another transgender male to female surgeon's site to douche 3 times a week, so we began that phase. It was the first item inside my vagina, but the douche nozzle slid inside relatively easy. It was neither painful nor pleasurable.

With the packing out, I had a week to spend with my neo-vagina before my follow-up appointment with Dr. Burke. I began feeling depressed and paranoid about how it was healing. I referred to it as 'if a hand grenade went off in my pants'. My labium were swollen, my left was puffier than my right, I had stitch marks, I had more vaginal discharge where I could feel it slowly dripping like a faucet, I read to use fragrance-free Dove soap for vaginal cleaning but I still had that 'medical' smell despite my OCD cleaning. I started Googling 'neo-vagina care' and stumbled upon 'Gender Critical' posts on reddit about neo-vaginas and transwomen and began hating myself for what I had done. Here was a sect of women who hated women like me. Who picked transwomen social media posts to 'discuss' in order to deplore our vaginas, calling them open-wounds, to state that our vaginas smell, call us fakes, use improper pronouns while referencing the post they were 'discussing', and just sounding like 'torch and pitchfork Nazi "feminists."'

I got the surgery to end my dysphoria because I am a woman too. I think it takes a lot of balls (pun intended) to have a surgeon take your 'patriarchal power', skin it like those apple peelers where the skin comes off in one long spiral piece, slice it in half like a hot dog, burn and roll it into a cavity in your pelvis, cut your scrotum open, castrate you, pull the entire spermatic cord out of your body, and burn and fold the scrotum into labia. So, either I'm certifiably insane with my 'autogynephilia' or I just want to be happy and be as physically identical as I can be to natal women.

My neo-vagina is similar enough to where we should be united as women regardless of backstory. My neo-vagina is healing but it's not an open wound for the rest of my life. I need to dilate because it's tight and I want to retain depth to avoid feeling like I'm being torn apart when I have sex. My dilation schedule for my first three months post-op was three times a day for ten minutes a session. So, oh em gee a big 'ole thirty minutes out of my day. At nine months to the rest of my life it's one or two times a week and sex can count as dilating. So, it's not some debilitating activity like in those Crohn's disease commercials where the girl is in the band and must shit when they are in studio and then on stage. It's not as strenuous as some transwomen make it sound and It's easy and not messy at all. I lay on a diaper changing pad, lube up, stick the dilator in, and listen to sports radio or play a game on my phone (omg

he listens to sports! Damn TIMS (Trans-identified **male**) invading sports! Real women don't like sports. (/r gendercritical).

I started gaining my confidence back by the end of week three of being post-op. My vulva was looking like, well, a vulva. The 'hand grenade' look was going away as my swelling went down. My urine stream was coming back under control and so I began peeing in the toilet again. The vaginal canal drippage slowed and didn't make me feel so dirty about myself. Did the discharge lessen because I kept clean or because I was healing? Or both? Bah! The trans-exclusionary radical feminists (TERFs) say that it'll always be dirty and will never heal regardless.

I had my follow-up appointment with Dr. Burke on a Thursday. A physician's assistant came in as I was laying bottomless with a sheet over me and checked my vaginal depth. She said I had "great depth" and wiped some leakage away. I felt embarrassed and apologized. I was still squeamish about my new body part. She said that I didn't need to apologize, that some discharge is normal because I was healing. Dr. Burke came in soon after and checked my depth also. He looked everything over and said that I was healing very nicely. I asked him when I could return to work.

"You can go back to work whenever you want," he said happily, "when do you want to go back? Tomorrow? How's tomorrow sound?" he was laughing at the end.

"Nooooo, that's a little too early," I retorted playfully.

"Well how about Monday then?" he asked.

"Yeah, that sounds good," I said, "now will I have any restrictions?"

He thought briefly, "Well no, it's going to be all up to how you feel. I'm not you so you're going to have to listen to your body. If you need to take a break then *take a break*," he finished with emphasis.

I nodded and smiled, "Ok fair enough. So, I won't touch F350s and stick to like Hyundai Elantras."

Dr Burke exited after we said our goodbyes, the physician's assistant came back with my dilator kit, gave me an instructional manual on how to use them, and I went to get my work note after we were finished.

PART 4

INTO THE HORIZON

Dated: November 2019- July 2020

I am dedicating this section to the people who support the future me and helped me soar:

My counselors Brianna and then Elizabeth who taught me empowerment and helped me develop self-esteem.

My manager Ricky for opening his mind up to people who are transgender and accepting us as people who can be good people. I thank you for supporting me with your understanding. Especially when I was recovering from surgery and in pain, bleeding, and needed to dilate.

My boyfriend James for being so down to earth and caring during my recovery process.

CHAPTER 1
Back in Black

I RETURNED TO an absolute wreck at work. The shop was a disaster area full of new and old tires, a ton of parts that needed to go back, and the floor needed to be swept in a bad way. I had returned to the start of the end of world aka. *Tire Season*. I worked 56 hours my first week back, but I noticed that I was less sore the more I worked. I changed my pad and went pee in the ladies' room instead of using the shop employee bathroom. When I was pre-op, I was constantly wiping piss and pubes off the seat with layers of tissue. I was joking with the boys before I left, and I vowed to never sit on that toilet seat ever again unless I purposely wanted to give myself a damn UTI. They thought I was funny. I thought it was gross.

However, the maxi pads were causing me discomfort. Perhaps it was because I had bought ones that were too thick, but they would bunch up in my underwear as if they were trying to make a paper airplane resulting in my vulva feeling squashed and drips of discharge running down the sides. I would get into a cloth adult brief with tapes when I got home, and the pain would immediately subside. Thankfully, James's mom had some packs of Depends Flex-fit pullups laying around and I made the switch to those. I instantly noticed the discharge nearly dissipating completely and the soreness around my vaginal canal greatly lessening.

I would dilate typically twice a day, though there were a few instances where I could only handle one time a day or where I felt ambitious and would go three times a day. The PA and Doctor Burke said that two times for fifteen minutes each was still ok. It is such a simple task that I fail to understand the misconception about it being some horrible chore or that our neo-vaginas will blast-door seal themselves unless you have a giant dildo in them 24/7. The PA instructed me to start with the smallest dilator. She also taught me that there are two ways to dilate. "Active dilation" is where you insert the dilator and manipulate it inside the vagina. You spin it inside you, or you can place your palm on the flat flared end and wiggle it in circles like an Atari joystick. "Passive dilation" is where you simply stick the dilator in and lay there or go make yourself a sandwich or something.

My kit contains five pink plastic phalluses with flared ends. She suggested at my first appointment to start with #2 since I had decent depth. After a month being post-op, I noticed that #2 offered little resistance and would slip right in. Perhaps it was because I was doing more "active dilation" versus "passive dilation". For future sessions I would start with #2 for two five-minute reps and then do #3 for about ten minutes to finish up. It was very difficult, and since I was still so fresh from surgery, I was unable to fit the entire dilator into my vaginal canal, but I was creating more girth and depth than with #2. I'd feel my vagina stretching and the resistance as I'd make millimeters of progress each dilation session. Let me dispel another myth about dilation. No, you are not "tearing apart tissue", you are stretching it. Not much different to when you're new at vaginal or anal sex. No, you do not bleed all over and make messes. I'd have a little spot of lube mixed with a tiny bit of discharge. Does it hurt? I'm sure everyone's mileage is different. For me, I would be sore afterwards especially on longer sessions. There were times where I would be reading and lose track of time. Oh? It's been a half hour already? (Oh my God that's so disgusting! You sat there with a plastic dildo covered in lube and puss inside your fake vagina for a half hour and didn't even notice? Gross!) [/r gendercritical].

All in all, I was doing well and looking forward to my check-up with Dr. Burke in a few months.

CHAPTER 2
Golden Splatters

By November, I was very pleased with how I was healing. I had a strip of skin slough where it looked like I had yellow-green putty stuck in between my inner labia. I was only mildly concerned since Dr. Burke uses the extra length of urethra to make a mucosa and the slough is just a result of healing. I changed from douching with Dove soap mixed with water to a solution of gold antibacterial soap and water. It took about a month before the slough finally shed off. It was sort of gross. It reminded me of peeling skin off a chicken. The slough rinsed off like little blups of fat and revealed a rosy red inner labium.

The overall pain was mitigating but I was still swollen, and it would feel nagging when I would run around and do a high volume of cars at work. The swelling greatly affected my urine stream. On my days off, I would pee relatively normally. I would just sit, keep my legs closed, and down it went but if I was sore, my urine stream would spray practically straight out, going over the bowl like I was playing a game at a state fair. This resulted in me yelling 'God dammit', trying to control my muscles to slow down the stream, and contorting myself to a position where I could make the stream into the bowl.

I was becoming depressed as this situation constantly occurred. How was I supposed to use the ladies' room in public if I always wound up peeing all over the place. How ladylike to hear 'God dammit' in a "man" voice and pee splattering all over the toilet?! I tried sitting all the way on the back of the seat. That didn't work. I tried sitting with my left leg open and my right leg normal. Nope. I tried it the other way. Nope. One time when I was at work, I sat down to pee in the ladies' room, closed my legs, and splatter paint the floor. It came out so forcefully like a firehose that I didn't even have time to react and reposition myself. So, I was like, "Ok this clearly isn't working with high accuracy. What if I just hover and bend right off the bat instead of doing it as a contingency plan?" That began working for the most part and I would only have to wipe a little overspray off the seat. Until I gave myself a golden shower... I was in my hover one potty trip, bent over at the waist and the overspray misted in my face.

The fear of never being able to pee correctly and therefore being unable to function in a public restroom caused me to console with James. He came up with an amazing idea.

"I don't know what I'm supposed to do," I bemoaned one evening after a bad day of peeing at work. "How are we supposed to go out on dates if I can't use a restroom? I just feel embarrassed like I'm a child or something. It's very disheartening"

James pondered my statement while staring at the television as most men do.

Later that evening I announced that I had to pee as perhaps women do. James chuckled and said "Damn Spiro" which was our ongoing joke since I would have to pee 1000 times after taking it. I entered the bathroom and was about to sit down when James came up the stairs.

"Here", he said as he handed me something from the doorway.

I looked at the object he handed me. He had taken a one-liter soda bottle and cut it in half creating a curved shield. "What the heck is this?" I said confused.

"It's a piss flapper," he answered matter-of-factly with his boyish smirk, "hold it between your legs when you pee." I looked at the shield in my hand and back down between my legs. "Come on, try it out."

I stuck the piss flapper between my legs. It fit comfortably and I started peeing. The stream came out forcefully but hit the flapper and angled right down into the toilet. No overspray, no wet thighs, no hovering, and no golden showers.

James looked pleased with himself and he grinned from the doorway. "Well?"

I smiled and was overjoyed. "You're so ingenious sometimes. My smart man! It certainly works. It feels comfortable and fits perfectly between my legs and the front of the toilet. It's nice to have some dignity back. That's what was causing me the most distress. Maybe this will help me learn the way I need to sit too."

James looked satisfied. "Well use that from now on, I'll see about making you a portable one."

I laughed and I finished blotting myself off, "Oh are we going to patent it and sell it on late-night TV?" I made my voice deeper and acted like a commercial, "Hi Billy Mayes here! Are you having trouble making your pee go in the toilet? Try the Piss Flapper 9000."

James feigned a serious look, "Maybe", and he turned to go back downstairs as I finished washing my hands.

CHAPTER 3
The Alpaca Bounce

My sex drive was starting to return the end of November to the beginning of December. Partly was that I was starting to think about how our first time would go and partly was because I was having sexy dreams. Even my self-conscious knew that I was a woman. I'd have lesbian dreams where I had my current parts, I'd have dreams where I was back in high school but the girls knew I was trans and let me in their cliques anyway, and I had dreams where I would walk into the guys locker-room and bolt back out.

I woke up one morning super aroused. I could feel this nagging feeling around my vulva extremely like the feeling I would get when I'd have an erection. I felt tingly, and my fuzzy blankets were sensual on my bare skin. It was my day off and so I began my dilating routine. My vaginal opening seemed tighter than usual and I twisted the dilator in a spiral to insert it. I felt different while dilating like I was being penetrated instead of performing a medical routine. I closed my eyes and let my mind wander. I began rapidly sliding the dilator in out of my vaginal canal and oh my Lord that felt good! I placed my palm on the flat end of the dilator and began bopping it in and letting it slide back out a bit before hitting it back into me. Faster and faster I slapped the dilator in my vagina and began moaning with pleasure. I felt an energy building up inside of me as my muscles quaked and I was ready to burst any second. Finally, the orgasm exploded from my body as I yelled out in ecstasy. My whole body shook rapidly, my consciousness tingled, and I felt a wave wash over me as I panted in pleasure.

As I came down from the rush of the orgasm, I noticed that physically I felt incomplete. I still needed a release. Perhaps a different kind this time? I gently tried to play with my clit, but I yelled out in a mixture of pain and pleasure. I was still extremely sensitive. I noticed that if I had a vehicle with a tight fit at work and bumped myself on a door or seat it would almost hurt with how sensitive I was. I became slightly frustrated as I lay in bed. I wanted to stimulate myself so badly! I grabbed a blanket and draped it over my genitals and tried with my hand. The feeling was still too much to take. I needed something softer.

I glanced over and my stuffed alpaca named Paxton was laid next to me. I grabbed it and began slowly grinding it over my clit to the top of my vaginal opening. Holy hell that felt amazing! I began pushing down a little more forcefully and the sensation increased. I closed my eyes and began masturbating. The energy began building up again and I began gently bouncing the stuffed animal off my clit. It felt fucking fantastic! Mixing in the grinding motion, I felt the energy build up inside me. Faster and faster I bounced the plushy off my clit until finally my body was so tense, ready to explode. My body stiffened and I screamed in pleasure! The orgasm was powerful, and my vulva seemed like it was pulsating as I moaned.

"Oh my God, oh my God, uhhhhh," I cried out. I felt a warm wetness dripping down my leg at my inner thigh as if I peed myself a little. "Holy shit," I whispered as I panted. My body felt exhausted and I laid there with my eyes closed for a minute as the wave of endorphins crashed over me. Finally, the rush ebbed, and I glanced over at my phone. I began shifting and getting up from bed. The wetness was still on my thigh and as I got out of bed, I gently poked the sheet where I was laying.

It was damp.

I was shocked.

I came while masturbating…

***

SINCE transwomen are born male, we have a prostate and what is known as the Cowper's glands. The glands sit next to the prostate and produce a clear liquid that travels out of the urethra. This is known as pre-cum in basic sexual vernacular.

"Bottom surgery" or a vaginoplasty for transwomen entails removal of the testes and spermatic cord but not the Cowper's or prostate. After surgery, the prostate acts as the g-spot for transwomen and transwomen have prostate exams performed through the neo-vagina.

Therefore, the sensation like I had dribbled pee when I came was technically pre-cum (if I still was physically male) yet it was cum none-the-less.

STILL awash in pleasure and amazement at my self-discovery, I began getting dressed to go to an appointment. Ironically, through all of this, I was scheduled to see Dr. Burke for my follow-up to see how I was healing. I chuckled to myself on how I would inform him of my "progress".

CHAPTER 4
The Lucky Sweater

I ARRIVED AT the hospital and waited in the clinic until I was called and taken to one of the rooms to get my vitals checked. The nurse was a cool older lady maybe late 40's and opened her binder and began typing my information into the computer.

"Any changes to your address or insurance," She asked me.

"Nope," I responded giddily.

"How tall are you?"

"Um, 5, 8," I answered.

The nurse nodded as she typed and moved the computer mouse, "Ok step up on the scale for me."

I hated scales because I felt that my weight gave me away as a transwoman. I stood on the scale as the nurse slid the weights across the bars. 140, 150, 160, fucking a…

"Ok you're 161," she concluded as she wrote it down in my chart.

"Dammit," I quietly said, "My goal is to stay under 160."

"Oh stop!" the nurse turned to me laughing, "You're so close. Try being older. I'm like 170!" I looked at her astonished. She didn't look 170 and was attractive. But she had no reason to lie.

"So how are things going hon," she asked holding my chart with her pen ready.

I smirked this goofy grin. "Well um, I want to tell you, but I don't know if it's TMI or not." I shifted in my chair.

The nurse waved her hand at me, "Oh lord, we're both women here. Tell me."

I took a breath and quickly thought of my reply. "I um, self-pleasured this morning and made my sheet wet." I smiled at the end.

The nurse chuckled, "That's great!" she exclaimed. "That's the kind of information we need to know and like to hear. Are you happy with your results?"

"Oh yeah," I nodded, "Whatever Dr. Burke ate or wore that day, tell him to do that every surgery."

The nurse laughed again, "Ok, well you tell him when you see him, follow me."

I followed her to the same room where I had my initial consultation and made my date.

The physician's assistant knocked and entered shortly after.

"Hi Joella, can you take off your jeans and underwear and let me take a look before the doctor comes in?"

I nodded, disrobed, and laid on the examining bed. She came over and looked at some parts of my vulva and gently moved my labium.

"How are things going?" she asked, "You look at little swollen still."

I nodded, "Yeah, if I'm moving around and doing a lot of lifting, I get sore but it's not terrible."

She nodded back, "Just be careful not to overdo it," she shifted her attention to my vaginal opening. She grabbed a gauze pad and wiped some discharge from my vagina.

I felt embarrassed, "I'm sorry," I said softly, "I cleaned after dilating this morning…"

She looked over at me, "it's totally ok, you're still healing and will have a little discharge. Let me go have Dr. Burke come in now." She left the room and a few minutes later I heard a knock on the door and Dr. Burke came into the examining room.

"Hi Joella! So how are things?" he said very chipper.

I chuckled, "Well, I don't know what you ate or if it was that sweater you wore the morning of my surgery, but you need to do that for every transgirl's surgery."

Dr. Burke raised an eyebrow, "Are you happy with your results then?" he seemed pleased with himself.

"Well…I um…self-pleasured myself and ejaculated," I said.

Dr. Burke smiled a wide grin, "So you ARE happy then. That's great to hear. May I have a quick peek?"

"Sure thing, you're the artist," I teased, "admire your work."

Dr. Burke sat on a stool in front of my open legs and looked around. He gently poked asking me how I was healing. He also mentioned that he noticed the swelling and that it would go down slowly but surely.

"You'll probably be all healed up sometime in February," he finished the exam with. "You can get dressed now, tell them up front to set you up for March. We'll take another look and discuss plans for a revision if you'd like."

"Ok, I will," I replied as I began moving to get off the examining bed. Dr. Burke and the physician's assistant collected their binders and left the room. I slowly got dressed, made my follow-up for March, walked to my car, and got in to drive home.

CHAPTER 5
"Open Wide"

I HAD MY first gynecological exam with Dr. Morrison in the beginning of March. I was extremely excited since she hadn't seen me in a little over a year. We were at the point in my transition where I would simply take the HRT as prescribed and to call her if anything serious changed with my mood or sex drive. I arrived at the office tired for a week's worth of work. My excitement kept me awake as I waited in the waiting room admiring the women's rights, fertility rights, and Stonewall art and posters as I've seen for the past 4 years of visits. This time though, they mattered to me more than before. Here I was, finally, a complete woman that I wanted to be. I was accepting of my sexuality where before I loathed transitioning.

Finally, I was called into the clinic to be weighed and have my vitals checked. I had gained a little weight since surgery, but I was still at my goal of under 160 pounds by a few pounds. Dr. Morrison entered and we began talking.

"So how are things?" She asked me with pen in hand.

"Everything went really well, and I've been back to work for 5 months now," I replied happily.

"Wow, it's been that long already?! How long were you out of work for?"

"4 weeks," I replied. "When I asked Dr. Burke if I could go back to work, he told me to just keep an eye on everything," I answered.

"That's great! So, recovery went well then?" she asked with a big smile.

"Yes, well, I'm still having to wear Depends pull-ups. Especially at work," I replied with an embarrassed look.

Dr. Morrison looked slightly confused. "Now is that for urinary incontinence or discharge?"

"I'm still having discharge," I answered meekly. "Particularly at work when I'm exerting myself a lot."

Dr. Morrison nodded. "Well you will be having a revision, right?"

I nodded back glancing down at my groin quickly. "I don't know," I started slowly, "I kind of like it the way it is, and I can't afford to get the revision."

Dr. Morrison looked concerned for a moment. "Well that's certainly up to you, it may go away as time passes. Remember that some discharge is normal for any vagina."

"Sure, sure," I nodded and then I grinned, "I really want you to see it. I hope that doesn't sound weird."

Dr. Morrison laughed, "It's not weird at all! I **am** your gynecologist after all. It's kind of what I do. I'll be honest I'm very excited to see it," she hesitated, "As long as you don't think that sounds weird," she glanced back at me. I chuckled. She opened a cabinet and handed me a thin blue cloth skirt with an elastic waist. "You get undressed and put that on. Let me go get someone to supervise the exam." Dr. Morrison departed the room and came back shortly with a nurse. Dr. Morrison slid some metal leg stirrups from under the examining bed. "Ok put your heels up here," she gestured to the stirrups, "and slide so your knees are bent."

I slid and placed my heels in the stirrups. Dr. Morrison lifted the top of the little skirt and began looking at my vagina.

"Yes, I see a little discharge," she said thoughtfully as she gently poked me in a few places. "How's your urine stream working out?" she asked with her head still looking at my ladybits.

"It goes all over the place most of the time," I replied. Dr. Morrison peeked her head out. "My boyfriend even made me a shield out of a soda bottle, so the stream bounces off. He calls it the piss flapper.

Dr. Morrison grinned and tilted her head back to examine me, "Yeah, I can see where it's a little uneven and the urethra looks a little pinched. It could be swelling or something he will want to address during the revision." She looked back up. "If you decide to have it of course."

I nodded.

"I just want to check your depth now and how things healed inside. Is that ok with you?" She asked.

I laughed, "Of course! After all you *are* my gynecologist."

She grabbed the long light on a bendy straw style swivel and pointed it down at my vagina. "Ok, this is a speculum, it is going to hold the vagina open so I can examine you."

I heard a little metal sound like spoons being lightly tapped together and then a stretching feeling on my vagina.

"Wow you have great depth here," she said amazed. She looked up smiling, "He did an amazing job."

I felt relieved as I slightly grimaced from the stretching feeling. "Yes, I think so too. I've had sex a few times now."

Dr. Morrison grinned, "Well that's good. That's part of it." She looked back down, and I felt a twisting of my genitals.

I slightly grimaced, "Oh, ow" I said softly.

"You're ok," Dr. Morrison said gently, "I just wanted to see more inside. You healed up great. You should be very happy with your results. Now relax for a second." I heard the "spoon sound" and the tension at my groin relaxed.

"Yes, I'm very happy, I even joked with Dr. Burke to keep that routine the morning of my surgery for every trans girl."

"ha, ha, good, good," she chuckled. "Well I want to do some lab work since it's been over a year. Any questions for me?"

I pondered, "I've been taking the HRT the same way as I was before surgery, shouldn't I change my doses?"

Dr. Morrison thought for a second, "No," she said matter-of-factly, "Keep taking everything as prescribed. We'll see if we have to make any changes when I get your lab work back."

"Ok," I answered bubbly and nodded.

"You can get dressed now," I'll go grab the request for bloodwork and meet you up front. She left the room and closed the door so I could change.

I was grinning like a fool while I was changing. The exam felt validating. I was a real woman. I mean I always was but not physically. "I had a vaginal exam!" my inner voice squealed with joy. "I had the thing in me that every woman hates, and it made me sore just like them!" I recomposed myself as I finished dressing and met Dr. Morrison at the front of the clinic to receive my lab work prescription.

I texted my friends Brittany and Andrea about my validating experience with the speculum.

CHAPTER 6
The Final Frontier

It is now July 8, 2020 and I am getting ready to wind down writing. I recently got promoted to store manager in May therefore receiving a nice raise and more responsibility. Well…most of the responsibilities I already had but now the onus fell more on me regarding how the shop operated. It felt like a victory to me that all the hard work for the past three years had paid off. That I was not going to become a statistic working in a quagmire position and being passed over for advancement.

I bought a new car to celebrate/ get rid of the two-door hatchback with ripped seat, mismatched window switch, and "fart-cannon" cat-back exhaust. It was time for a car that a 35-year-old professional would drive. However, I ran into a snag after buying the car. My trade-in was registered to my deadname and I registered the new car in my legal name, so the DMV was flagging it as if I traded in someone else's car. I needed my name change court order to prove that I was who owned the trade-in. The problem was that NY state still had it because you have to send in the court order to change the name on your birth certificate and who knew how long it would take to get back with the Covid-19 pandemic going on.

Then a blessing happened. My birth certificate arrived the day after the salesmen informed me that he needed the paperwork.

I opened up the birth certificate paperwork and scanned it over. Surprisingly, I didn't cry or fawn over the change. Perhaps it was the length of time that it took to arrive, but I was still content and relieved that the final piece of my transition was complete. Seeing "Joella Sylvia Laramay", "sex: female", and my parents' names was soothing and validated that I was "born" into the wrong sex and that transitioning was a lifesaving decision.

I could have changed the birth certificate when I changed my driver's license, but I wanted to wait until after surgery. All you do is send in an amendment form stating why you are changing the birth certificate and send in the name change court order if you are changing your name on the certificate too. It was also free. Imagine that.

All in all, I am now complete. I am able to live my life now without hating my body and mind. I go out in public and get gendered correctly. I still squeal inside when someone calls me her, she, miss, or ma'am. I still have funny moments like when a man opens a door for me, and I hesitate as they wait for me to enter. I used to worry that they knew I was trans and were just being polite. But I'll always be different and if they know that I'm trans that's ok as long as they're respectful. We're all different. I'll be a lot more different than say another cis woman to cis woman but it's ok to me. I am proud to be who I am and now proud to be trans because it takes strength and courage to transition and be yourself. You are not only fighting with yourself but with the societal "norms" that make you have the self-doubt in the first place.

James and I are still together and going strong through all of my transitioning. When we first started dating, he had said that no matter what path I chose he would support me, and he certainly has. We have become great friends and love each other very much.

My parents on the other hand have not reached out and I don't think they ever will. I have tried to call them with no answer or reply and have even debated on visiting them during a work vacation. Yet without feeling wanted, my fear would be that they would turn me away from their home. The sadness of the situation has slowly dissipated as I've come to terms that it's not something that I can control and that the problem rests with them, not with me.

Overall, it is my hope that the world continues to progress, and people can live their true lives with support and without fear of violence, discrimination, and fear. We only get one life so let's love and respect one another for who they truly are.

www.ingramcontent.com/pod-product-compliance
Lightning Source LLC
Chambersburg PA
CBHW071429070526
44578CB00001B/50